Scandinavian Glass
1930-2000
Fire & Sea

Leslie Piña
&
Lorenzo Vigier

Schiffer Publishing Ltd

4880 Lower Valley Road, Atglen, PA 19310 USA

Dedication

To my sister, Rita, my brother-in-law, Javier and my wonderful
nephews, Javier Andre and Lorenzo Javier.
—Lorenzo

For the artists and designers of Scandinavian glass.
—Leslie

Designed by Leslie Piña
Layout by Mark David Bowyer
Type set in Korinna BT / Korinna BT

ISBN: 0-7643-2449-7
Printed in China
1 2 3 4

Published by Schiffer Publishing Ltd.
4880 Lower Valley Road
Atglen, PA 19310
Phone: (610) 593-1777; Fax: (610) 593-2002
E-mail: Info@schifferbooks.com

For the largest selection of fine reference books on this and
related subjects, please visit our web site at
www.schifferbooks.com
We are always looking for people to write books on new and
related subjects. If you have an idea for a book please contact
us at the above address.

This book may be purchased from the publisher.
Include $3.95 for shipping.
Please try your bookstore first.
You may write for a free catalog.

In Europe, Schiffer books are distributed by
Bushwood Books .
6 Marksbury Ave.
Kew Gardens
Surrey TW9 4JF England
Phone: 44 (0) 20 8392-8585; Fax: 44 (0) 20 8392-9876
E-mail: info@bushwoodbooks.co.uk
Free postage in the U.K., Europe; air mail at cost.

Contents

Part II

Acknowledgments

We would like to thank the following individuals, companies, and institutions for their support and generous help with the completion of this book. Without them, this project would not have been possible.

Carol Jo Williams
Ramón Piña
Paivi Jantunen at iittala
Kosta Boda
Ulf Rosen at Lindshammar
Mats Jonasson Maleras
Ake Ernstsson at Sea Glasbruk
Tiina Willman
Eva-Pia Worland
Anne Palkonen
Michael Ellison
Gordon Harrell
Trond Einar Indsetviken
Robert Khoury
The Rakow Library at The Corning Museum of Glass
Ursuline College Library

Introduction

Twentieth-century Scandinavian glass is remarkably varied. Early in the century a restrained modernism resulted in primarily colorless glass that depended on form and surface decoration. The technical virtuosity of the engraver and cutter was as critical as that of the glassblower.

As the century progressed, tastes turned toward color. While some designers experimented with internal decoration in blown glass, others invented playful forms that required molds for their execution. In both cases, color was central, and designers' imaginations had no boundaries.

In most cases, the function, the usefulness, still exemplified Scandinavian glass. In some instances, however, experiments with sculptural forms consciously ignored this fundamental tenet of modernism and requirement of decorative art — *function*. Flygsfors, and even some Holmegaard designs, clearly broke out away from pure functionalism. Even factory-produced glass broke away from the "decorative art" label. This sculptural and necessarily one-of-a-kind glassware was indisputably fine art — *without function*.

Glassware for the table was created by the same designers responsible for vases, figural forms, and other purely decorative

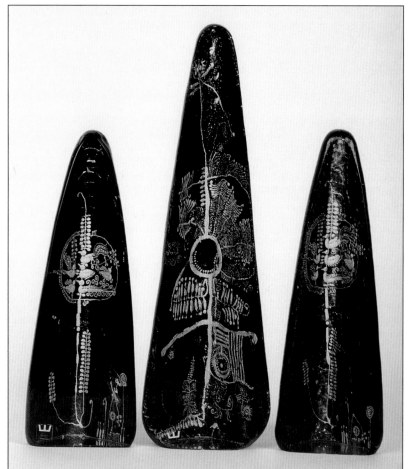

items. The examples shown in this book include well-designed functional tableware, some surprisingly useful art, plus beautiful, though "useless," art. (There is nothing bad about uselessness.)

This volume, entitled *Fire & Sea*, is about modern Scandinavian glass that depends on color for its success. Forms vary from the utterly simple to the outrageously complex. The separate volume, entitled *Smoke & Ice*, includes examples of glass by many of the same designers and companies— but without the color. Since designers and makers looked to nature for inspiration, the titles reflect her elements. Whether your taste leans toward the crisp and icy or the liquid and fiery, the decades of Scandinavian design leadership provides a smorgasbord for all.

A word about pricing

As with any book with a price guide, this should be looked at with some caution. Price ranges and prices vary, and each transaction is unique. Any guide can only suggest a range based on a sample of specific sellers and buyers. We have used a variety of sources to arrive at the numbers in this guide: auction catalogs, on-line auctions, shows, shops, flea markets, web sites, companies, and individuals. Some items are relatively rare, and fewer transactions have occurred. Others are fairly common, so it was much easier to identify a reasonable price range. National and regional differences, seasonal changes, and other factors can create prices outside of the suggested range. Condition is extremely important. Unlike furniture, which should show some wear and signs of use, glass cannot. Chips, cracks, fogginess (sick glass) or other damage will cause a piece of glass to lose much, perhaps all, of its monetary value. Rim chips can often be repaired (ground) without causing devaluation, providing the piece does not become noticeably shorter. The only acceptable sign of wear would be surface scratches on the bottom where a vase or a bowl sits on a hard surface. These minute scratches are "good" signs of age, and they cannot be imitated any more than patina on wood.

So the prices suggested in this volume are approximate and should be handled with care. Transactions outside the range are to be expected. Neither the authors nor the publisher can be responsible for any outcome from using the price guide, but we hope that the information offered will be helpful to your collecting, edification, and pleasure.

Chapter 1 • Simple

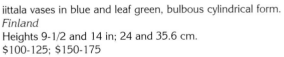
iittala vases in blue and leaf green, bulbous cylindrical form. *Finland*
Heights 9-1/2 and 14 in; 24 and 35.6 cm.
$100-125; $150-175

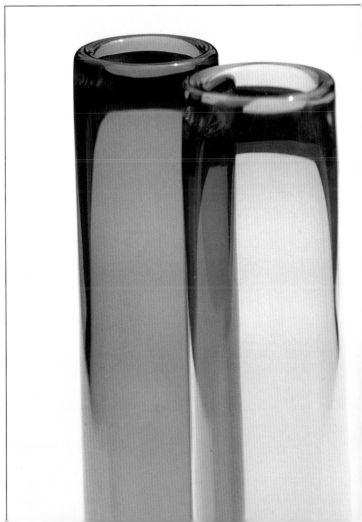

Holmegaard blown cylindrical vases in steel blue and leaf green glass, with heavy bottoms, designed by Per Lutken in 1957 and shown in the "Glass 1959" exhibit at Corning, signed. *Denmark*
Height 14-3/4 in; 37.5 cm.
$150-200 each

Holmegaard cylindrical vases designed by Per Lutken in 1957-1958. The taller and slightly tapered design is from the "Labrador" series, signed. *Denmark*
Height 14-1/2 and 6 in; 36.8 and 15.2 cm.
$150-200; $75-100

Kastrup and Holmegaard vases. Holmegaard leaf green bulbous bottle with narrow neck designed by Christer Holmgren around 1963, signed; Kastrup "Capri" steel blue vase designed by Jacob Bang in 1962, of tall cylindrical form with flared rim; and leaf green cylindrical vase with weighted base designed by Per Lutken in 1957, signed. *Denmark*
Heights 10 in, 14 in, and 9 in; 25.4, 35.6, and 22.9 cm.
$125-200 each

iittala leaf green beaker pitcher with flattened bulbous bottom and elongated cylindrical neck, designed by Timo Sarpaneva, signed. *Finland*
Height 10 in; 25.4 cm.
$225-250

iittala i-400 (straight) and i-401 (round) "bird bottle" flasks in blue and leaf green glass, from the i-collection (or i-lasi, i-glass, i-color) designed by Timo Sarpaneva in 1956, signed. *Finland*
Heights 7-1/2 and 6-1/2 in; 19 and 16.5 cm.
$225-300 each

Gullaskruf leaf green and steel blue bulbous beaker pitchers, probably designed by Arthur Percy ca. 1960. *Sweden*
Height 11-1/2 in; 29.2 cm.
$250-350 each

Nuutajarvi Notsjo "Soap Bubble" vases, of simple globular forms in clear and mossy green glass, designed by Kaj
Frank in 1950, in production from 1951 to 1961. *Finland*
$400-600 each

Photo courtesy of iittala

iittala leaf green slightly bulbous
cylindrical vases cased in clear
glass with paperweight base, one
with acid matte finish, from the
"Lappi" series, designed by Erkki
VeSanto in 1958, and produced
from 1963 to 1968, signed.
Finland
Height 6 in; 16.25 cm.
$100-150 each

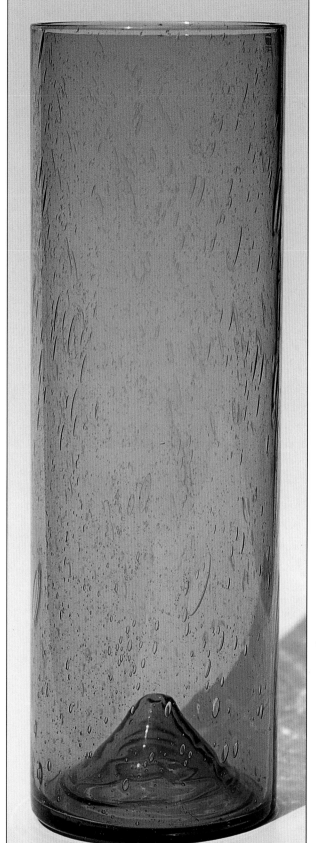

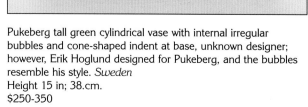

Pukeberg tall green cylindrical vase with internal irregular
bubbles and cone-shaped indent at base, unknown designer;
however, Erik Hoglund designed for Pukeberg, and the bubbles
resemble his style. *Sweden*
Height 15 in; 38.cm.
$250-350

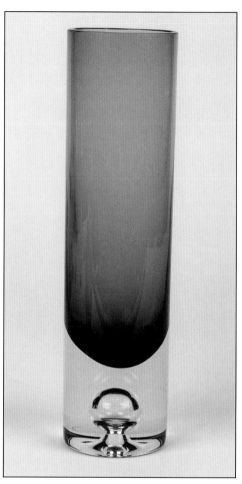

iittala blue cylindrical vase cased in crystal with
paperweight base and single large bubble,
designed by Tapio Wirkkala, ca. 1960, signed.
Finland
Height 9-3/8 in; 23.8 cm.
$225-300

Three Aseda tapered cylindrical vases designed by Bo Borgstrom, cased in clear glass with paperweight base and single large bubble; leaf green, red, and amber, ca. 1960s. *Sweden*
Height 9 in; 22.9 cm.
$60-80 each

Sea Glasbruk vase with bulbous cylindrical form in honey glass, with heavy base, ca. 1960. *Sweden*

Smalandshyttan vases with bulbous forms in light blue and raspberry pink glass, with heavy bases. *Sweden*

Heights 6 in, 7 in, 7-3/4 in; 15.25, 17.8, and 19.7 cm.
$30-40 small, $100-150 each

Strombergshyttan droplet vases in amethyst cased in clear glass with paperweight bases, designed by Gunnar Nylund ca. 1957, signed.
Sweden
Heights 8-1/4 and 9-3/4 in; 21 and 24.8 cm.
$200-250 each

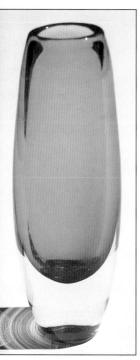

Smalandshyttan raspberry pink bulbous cylindrical vase cased in clear glass, with paperweight base.
Sweden
Height 7-3/4 in; 19.7 cm.
$100-150

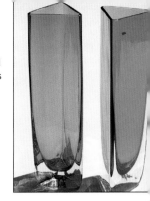

Lindshammar triangular vases in turquoise cased in clear glass, designed by Gunnar Ander ca. 1958. These vases were imported by the American company, Fostoria. *Sweden*
Height 11 in; 28 cm.
$100-125 each

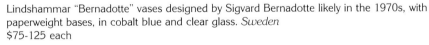

Lindshammar "Bernadotte" vases designed by Sigvard Bernadotte likely in the 1970s, with paperweight bases, in cobalt blue and clear glass. *Sweden*
$75-125 each

Photo courtesy of Lindshammar

IFP mossy green vase with bulbous form cased in clear glass, labeled. Note that this design was originally made by Sea Glasbruk. *Sweden*

Three Aseda vases in mossy green with clear paperweight bases, one with large air bubble designed by Bo Borgstrom, ca. 1960s. *Sweden*

Heights 6 to 12 in; 15.25 and 30.5 cm.
$30-40 small; $60-80 each

Opposite:
Gullaskruf gray-blue vase cased in clear glass designed by Arthur Percy ca. 1958. This vase was selected for the Corning Glass Museum Special Exhibition "Glass 1959" due to its excellent design. *Sweden*

Strombergshyttan vases in amethyst and gray, cased in clear glass, with paperweight bases, designed by Gunnar Nylund ca. 1957, signed. *Sweden*

Heights 7-1/2 in, 10-1/4 in, 6 in; 19, 26, and 15.24 cm.
$150-250 each

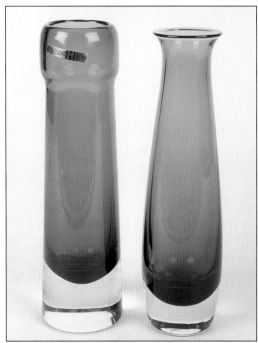

Holmegaard bulbous and
cylindrical vases in deep blue,
designed by Per Lutken, ca. 1957
and 1960. *Denmark*
Heights 8-1/2 and 7 in; 21.6 and
17.78 cm.
$125-200 each

Hadeland vases in a coffee brown glass
underlay and heavy clear glass bases.
Heights 8-1/4 in, 8 in; 21 and 20.3 cm.
$60-80 each

Aseda vases designed by Bo Borgstrom
ca. 1960s of cylindrical form with bulbous
bases, amber and leafy green. *Sweden*
Heights 8 in; 20.3 cm.
$60-80 each

Riihimaen Lasi vases designed by Nanny Still.
"Koristepullo" vase designed in 1959, in the flat rim
variant of the series, produced from 1959 to 1968,
signed. *Finland*
"Meripihka" vase designed in 1953 with biomorphic
form, signed. *Finland*
Heights 12-1/2 in, 3-1/4 in; 31.75 and 8.25 cm.
$300-400 each

Top Left:
Kosta vases designed by Vicke Lindstrand ca. 1965, in an earthy brown to sea blue gradient, with a single suspended bubble in the clear glass base, signed. *Sweden*
Height 8-3/4 in; 22.25 cm.
$300-400 each

Bottom:
Riihimaen Lasi (Riihimaki) vases in different colors and same form with tapered top and bottom, ca. 1970s. *Finland*
Height 10 in; 25.4 cm.
$80-120 each

Top Right:
Amethyst Riihimaki vase *(Finland)* next to similar form made by Aseda, designed by Bo Borgstrom. *(Sweden)* Notice that the Aseda form is slightly more bulbous and less linear.

Variety of transparent colors and sizes of lightweight bottle vases made mostly in Sweden by Gullaskruf (designed by Arthur Percy in 1952), Aseda, Elme, Lindshammar and others.
Heights range from 9-3/4 to 27 in; 24.75 to 68.5 cm.
$75-150 each depending on height and color (27-inch piece $250-350)

Gullaskruf bottle vases designed by Arthur Percy in 1952, in blue charcoal glass. This form was selected for the Corning Glass Museum Special Exhibition of 1959 due to its excellent design. *Sweden* Heights 15-1/2 in, 20 in, 12 in; 39.4, 50.8, and 30.5 cm. $75-150 each depending on height

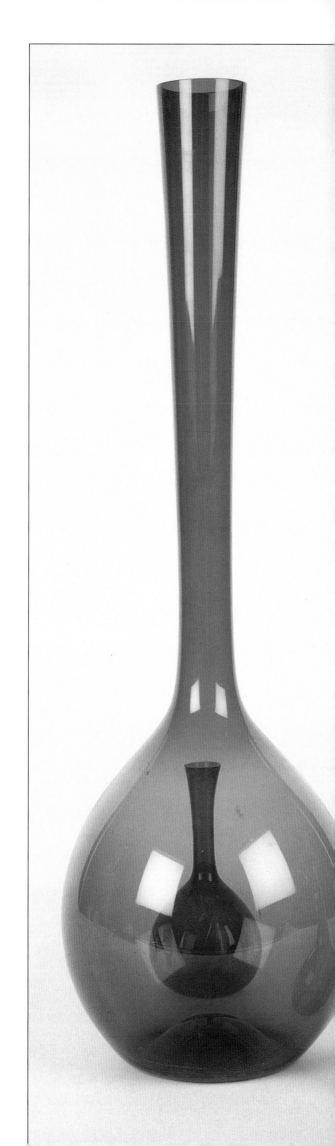

The 2 smaller vases, one with flattened sides, and the other with the "deflated" center are Elme designs. *Sweden*

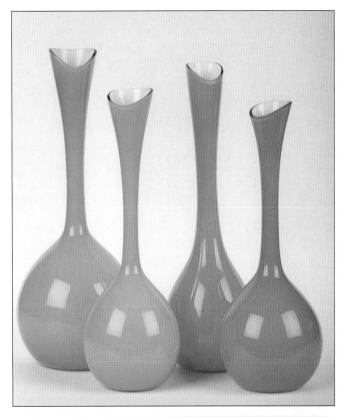

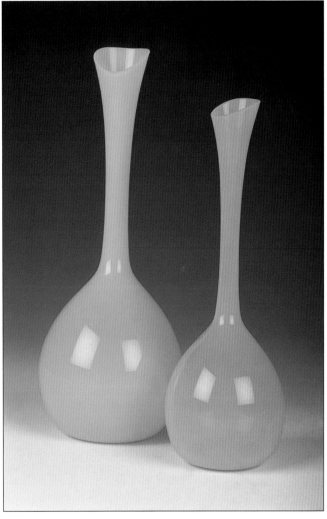

Lindshammar cased opaque bottle vases, designed by Gunnar Ander ca. 1958, with slightly flared and cut rims, very light weight, label. *Sweden*
Heights 9-1/2 to 11-1/4 in; 24.1 and 28.6 cm.
$125-175 each

Lindshammar bottle vases, designed by Gunnar Ander, in featherweight opalescent sun yellow. *Sweden*
Heights 8-1/2 and 9-1/2 in; 21.6 and 24.1 cm.
$125-175 each

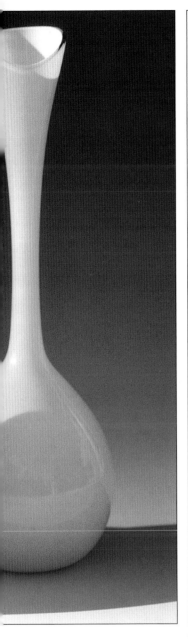

Heavy opaque vases with flat flared rims: left, blood red, designed by Kaj Franck for Nuutajarvi Notsjo in 1975 *(Finland)*; and right in royal blue by Plus Glasshytte of Norway, ca. 1970s, signed.
Heights 7 and 5 in; 18 and 12.5 cm.
$300-400 and $200-300

Lindshammar cased bottle designed by Gunnar Ander and imported by Fostoria Glass in West Virginia.
Sweden
Height 9 in; 22.9 cm.
$125-175

Top Left:
Holmegaard cased opaque cylindrical vases with flared lip, in black and orange over white, designed by Michael Bang in 1971. *Denmark*
Heights 7 and 9-1/4 in; 17.8 and 12.7 cm.
$150-200 each

Bottom Left:
Holmegaard gulvases in blue, red, and yellow cased over white. *Denmark*
Heights 10, 12, and 14 in; 25.4, 30.5, and 35.5 cm.
$150-400 each depending on height

Top Right:
Holmegaard gulvases from the "Pallet" series in chrome yellow, designed by Michael Bang in 1968 (after a transparent design by Otto Bauer in 1962), shown with white Italian vase with chrome yellow bubble stopper. Holmegaard vases in this "Pallet" series sometimes used this type of stopper as well. *Denmark*
Heights 10 and 14 in; 25.4 and 35.5 cm.
$150-250 and $300-400

Bottom Right:
Gulvases in red cased on white. *Denmark*

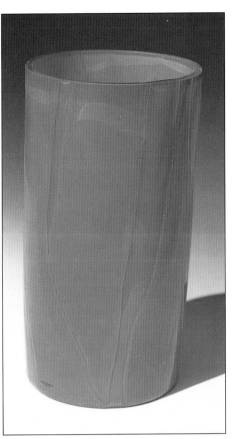

Cased cylindrical vases: left, Aseda designed by Bo Borgstrom ca. 1960s, khaki green with rolled rim; right, Lindshammar orange and yellow opalescent, designed by Gosta Sigvard ca.1970s, signed. *Sweden*
Heights 8 and 7-1/2 in; 20.3 and 19 cm.
$100-125 and $200-250

Kosta Boda monochromatic cased vase in opaque turquoise, with subtle texture, designed by Anna Ehrner in 1999, cellophane label. *Sweden*
Height 12-1/2 in; 31.75 cm.
$250-350

Lindshammar vase designed by Gunnar Ander around the late 1960s with an organic droplet form and a dark amber underlay, cased in yellow honey glass. *Sweden*
Height 9 in; 22.9 cm.
$250-350

Aseda cylindrical vase in opalescent yellow cased in clear, designed by Bo Borgstrom ca. 1960s. *Sweden*
Height 12-1/2 in; 31.75 cm.
$100-125

Lindshammar heavy cased bubble vase, designed by Gunnar Ander around the late 1960s, in pale honey color, with blown sculptural effect around the base of the neck, signed. *Sweden*
Height 7-1/4 in; 18.4 cm.
$200-250

Chapter 2 • Complex

iittala "Atlas" designed by Harri Koskinen in 1996, tall candleholders with elongated water-tower form in various colors. *Finland*
$75-90 depending on color

Photos by Markku Alatalo courtesy of iittala

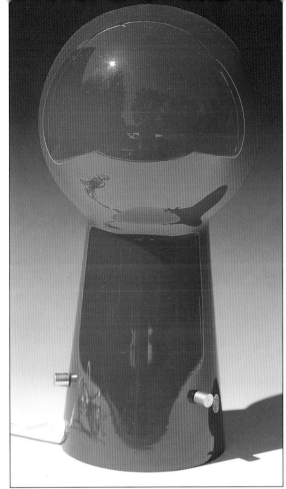

Laurel lamp with cased red-orange water-tower
form made in Sweden.
Height 13 in; 33 cm.
$250-350

Blue glass blown into textured copper form,
probably from Finland.
Height 6-1/2 in; 16.5 cm.
$200-300

Aseda vases designed by Bo Borgstrom ca. 1960s, in a variety of complex and geometric shapes and sizes, in vibrant cased color combinations, some including Bo Borgstrom's traditional open and suspended bubble base, as well as dimpled bases. All Aseda vases are labeled rather than signed. *Sweden*
Heights 6 in to 12 in; 15.25 and 30.5 cm.
$60-150 each depending on color, complexity, and size.

In most cases the Riihimaki cased mold-blown pieces are heavier and of finer quality than Aseda; these Riihimaki usually have polished rims, while Aseda are hot finished.

Riihimaen Lasi vase in deep aquamarine glass cased in clear glass, with a protruded ring at mid-top, found in the export catalog of 1976. *Finland* Aseda vases in purple and amber glass, cased in clear glass, designed by Bo Borgstrom ca. 1960s. *Sweden* Average heights 10 in; 25.4 cm. $60-100 each

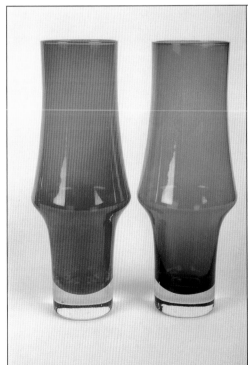

Riihimaen Lasi vases in green and orange glass cased in clear glass, with mid-gurgle and tapered top, found in the export catalog of 1976. *Finland* Height 9-3/4 in; 24.75 cm. $75-100 each

Riihimaen Lasi "Solmuke"(Knot) vases designed by Tamara Aladin in forest green and cobalt blue glass, with 2 gurgles or knots, cased in clear glass. *Finland* Heights 10 in and 8 in; 25.4 and 20.2 cm. $150-200 each

"Pagoda" vase designed by Nanny Still in 1968, in olive green glass cased in clear glass. *Finland*

"Solmuke" (Knot) vase designed by Tamara Aladin in olive green glass, cased in clear glass. *Finland*

Aseda ringed vases in amber and orange glass cased in clear glass, designed by Bo Borgstrom ca. 1960s. *Sweden*

Heights 8-1/2 to 9-3/4 in; 21.6 to 24.75 cm. $100-200 each

Riihimaen Lasi gurgled vases in ruby red glass, cased in clear glass, found in the 1976 export catalog. *Finland*
Heights 8 to 12 in; 20.2 to 30.5 cm.
$100-300 each, depending on size

Riihimaen Lasi vases in turquoise glass and amethyst, cased in clear glass, designed by Tamara Aladin, ca. 1970. *Finland*
Heights 8 to 12 in; 20.2 to 30.5 cm.
$100-300 each, depending on size

Riihimaen Lasi vases in olive glass, cased in clear glass, ca. 1970. *Finland*
The first vase is from the "Ruusu" (Rose) series, designed by Tamara Aladin, ca. 1972.
Heights 8 to 12 in; 20.2 to 30.5 cm.
$100-300 each, depending on size and complexity

Above and below:
Riihimaki vases in teal and amethyst in rocket or lamp shape, designed by Aimo Okkolin, ca. 1960s, some acid stamped and numbered 1436. *Finland*
Heights 5 to 8 in; 12.7 to 20.2 cm.
$125-225 each

Riihimaen Lasi vases in olive glass, cased in clear glass, ca. 1970. *Finland*
Heights 8 to 12 in; 20.2 to 30.5 cm.
$100-300 each, depending on size and complexity

Top Left:
Amethyst lampshade made in Sweden,
on brass base designed by Hans Agne
Jakobsson, label.
Height 13-1/2 in; 34. 3 cm.
$400-600

Nuutajarvi Notsjo hourglass vase in
deep cobalt, with label. *Finland*
Height 11 in; 27.94 cm.
$200-300

Nuutajarvi Notsjo vases designed by Kaj Franck in hourglass form.
This design was in production from 1957 to 1969. *Finland*
$400-500 each

Photo courtesy by Timo Kauppila of iittala

Riihimaki vases in red and green, turned spindle form, found in the export catalog of 1976. *Finland*
Height 11 in; 28 cm.
$200-250 each

Alsterfors cased orange vases in blocky turned spindle form. *Sweden*
Height 8 in; 20.3 cm.
$60-80 each

Aseda vases designed by Bo Borgstrom in opalescent orange cased in clear glass, ca. 1960s. *Sweden*
Heights 5 to 12 in; 12.7 to 30.5 cm.
$100-200 each, depending on size and complexity

Aseda vases designed by Bo Borgstrom in opalescent yellow
(one in red) cased in clear glass, ca. 1960s. *Sweden*
Heights 5 to 12 in; 12.7 to 30.5 cm.
Low bowl/vase diameter 6-3/4 in; 17.2 cm.
$100-200 each, depending on size and complexity

Holmegaard "Carnaby" vases, designed by Per Lutken, and "Pallet" vase designed by Michael Bang, both in red cased over opaque white, designed in 1968. Kastrup Holmegaard labels. *Denmark*
Heights 12 and 13 in; 30.5 and 33 cm.
$200-300 each

Kosta Boda "Hot Pink" ribbed cased vases designed by Ann Wahlstrom in 2000, with hot pink, yellow, and blue interiors. *Sweden*
Photo courtesy of Kosta Boda

Elme cased melon-form vases with long narrow neck, red and blue cased over white. *Sweden*
Height 9-1/2 in; 24.1 cm.
$100-125 each

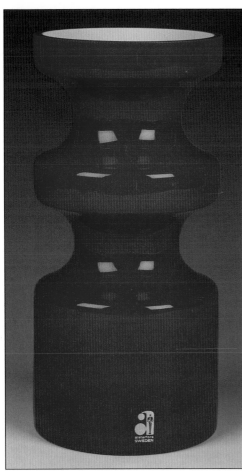

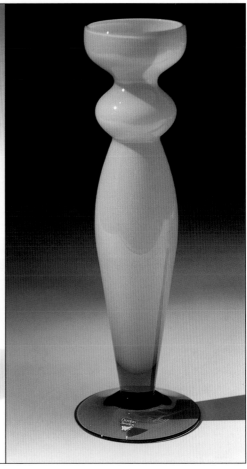

Alsterfors cased vase in red-orange over white, with label, likely designed by P. O. Strom in the late 1960s. *Sweden*
Height 7-1/2 in; 19.cm.
$100-125

Aseda cased vase in blue over white, designed by Bo Borgstrom, with label, ca. 1960s. *Sweden*
Height 5-1/2 in; 14 cm.
$60-80

Orrefors cased vase in green over white, with label. ca. 1990s. *Sweden*
Height 10-1/2 in; 26.7 cm.
$100-150

Boda-Afors blue vase in complex shape, designed by Bertil Vallien in the mid-1960s, with paper label denoting his name, unsigned. This is an example of Vallien's early work. *Sweden*
Height 10 in; 25.4 cm.
$250-300

Dansk smoky tone vase, made in Sweden.
Height 8 in; 30.2 cm.
$75-100

Riihimaen Lasi Oy (Riihimaki) "Tornado" vase designed by Tamara Aladin in the late 1960s, in green complex form, signed. *Finland*
Height 8 in; 30.2 cm.
$175-225

Nuutajarvi Notsjo "Pikku-majakka" (little lighthouse) candleholder vases, designed by Oiva Toikka and produced from 1960 to 1970, in amber brown glass, Arabia label and Nuutajarvi Notsjo signature. *Finland*
Height 9-1/4 in; 23.5 cm.
$200-300 each

Magnor green candleholders with clear stem and foot, label.
Norway
Height 6 in; 15.25 cm.
$30-40 each

iittala "Novitas" vase, designed by Timo Sarpaneva in 1965, complex form in apple green, signed TS. *Finland*
Height 6 in; 15.25 cm.
$250-300

Dansk candleholders designed by Jens Quistgaard in green molded complex from, Denmark, with molded signature.
Height 2-1/2 in; 6.4 cm.
$15-25 each

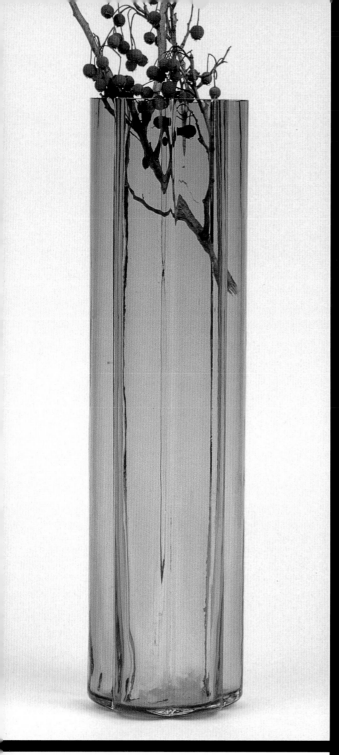

Dansk tall slender reeded vase
designed by Jens Quistgaard, in teal.
Height 14 in; 35.5 cm.
$100-150

Diameter 11 in; 28 cm.
$100-150

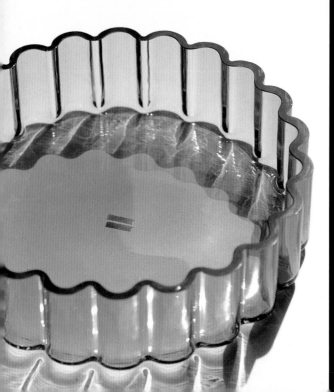

Large flat teal bowl with same reeded pattern,
attributed to Jens Quistgaard for Dansk, with
label Finland.
Diameter 11 in; 28 cm.
$100-150

iittala vase designed by Tapio Wirkkala in 1958, in lilac with clear base. *Finland*
Height 5-1/4 in; 13.5 cm.
$200-300

Kosta Boda tiered and tapered "Mezzo" vases in pale lilac, designed by Ann Wahlstrom in 1987, signed. This design won the award for "Excellent Swedish Design" in 1988.
Sweden
Heights 6 and 8 in; 15 and 20 cm.

Different light effect.

Chapter 3 • Cut

Blue Swedish optic vase
with engraved male nude,
possibly by Johansfors.
Sweden
Height 7-1/2 in; 19 cm.
$300-400

Detail.

Karhula vase with deeply cut
rings and stars in light teal,
designed by Goran Hongell
likely in late 1930s or 1940s,
signed G. Hongell Karhula.
Finland
Height 6 in; 15.25 cm.
$350-400

Cut and sandblasted bowl in deep teal blue with abstract symbols, not signed, possibly Swedish.
Diameter 6-3/4 in; 17 cm.
$100-150

Karhula vase in light emerald green with delicate cut design of figures holding hands under a tree, signed TL Karhula. *Finland*
Height 6 in; 15.25 cm.
$150-200

Karhula bowl in pale green with delicate cut underwater scene, likely designed in late 1930s or 1940s. *Finland*
Diameter 9-1/2 in; 24 cm.
$200-250

Karhula vase designed by Frans Rantinen, ca. late 1930s, in pale green with delicate cut design of figure cutting down a tree, signed FR Karhula. *Finland*
Height 8 in; 20.3 cm.
$200-250

Karhula bowl designed by Goran Hongell likely in late 1930s or 1940s, in pale green with delicate cut stars design, signed G. Hongell Karhula. *Finland*
Diameter 6 in; 15.25 cm.
$150-200

Nuutajarvi Notsjo "Prisma" vase designed by
Kaj Franck in four-sided flattened diamond
form with purples blending into blues. *Finland*
$800-1200

Photo by Timo Kauppila courtesy of iittala

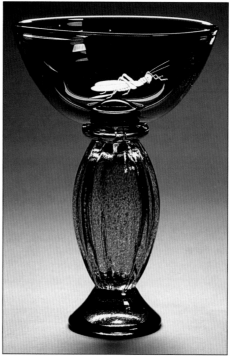

Nuutajarvi Notsjo "Prisma" vase designed by Kaj
Franck in four-sided flattened diamond form with
greens blending into blues, signed. This series was
in production from 1954 to 1968. *Finland*
Height 6-1/4 in; 16 cm.
$600-800

Kosta Boda Atelier "Semiramis" pedestal bowl
designed by Gunnel Sahlin in 1991, in bold
amethyst and green speckled glass, with an
engraved grasshopper on the transparent
amethyst glass top. *Sweden*
$400-500

Photo courtesy of Kosta Boda

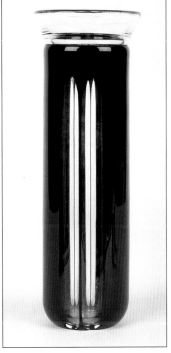

Kosta facet cut teardrop form in the "Ventana" technique, of amber glass cased in clear, designed by Mona Morales-Schildt in 1960, signed. *Sweden*
Height 6-1/2 in; 16.5 cm.
$600-800

Kosta Boda "Seaside" vase, heavy-walled cylindrical form with sliced angular rim, in clear glass with cobalt blue vertical bands, designed by Goran Warff in 1998, signed. *Sweden*
Height 9-1/2 in; 24.1 cm.
$250-300

Orrefors cased cylindrical vase in charcoal black with four deep vertical fluted cuts, designed by Klas-Goran Tinback ca. 1982, signed. *Sweden*
Height 10-1/4 in; 26 cm.
$250-300

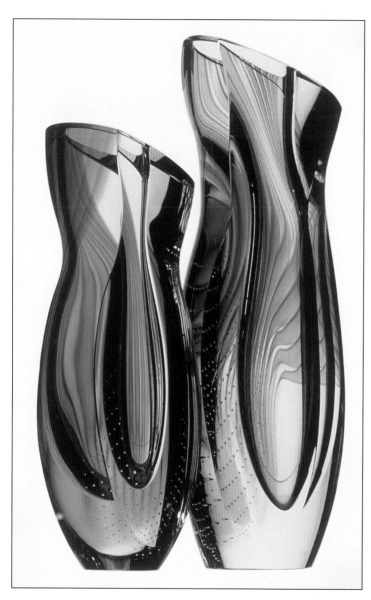

Kosta Boda "Naxos" vases designed by Goran Warff. Limited edition 2000, with deep ocean colors and diagonally slices rims. *Sweden*

Photo courtesy of Kosta Boda

iittala Pro Arte "Lago" series designed by Kerttu Nurminen in 2000 in cobalt blues, showing tall and short cylindrical vases and geode form bowl.

Photo by Timo Kauppila courtesy of iittala

Top Left:
Kosta "Bibelot" in the "Ventana" technique, of triple cased and facet cut glass in hot pink, yellow, and orange, designed by Mona Morales-Schildt in 1963. "Bibelot" is a series of small sculptures in cylindrical shapes with different and complex surface cuts (Ventana), which expose the layers of coloring. *Sweden*
Height 3 in; 7.6 cm.
$400-600

Bottom Left:
Kosta cube paperweight designed by Mona Morales-Schildt ca. 1960s, with internal layers of orange and raspberry pink glass and rounded corners, signed. *Sweden*
Height 1-3/4 in; 4.5 cm.
$300-400

Top Right:
Bottom view.

Bottom Right:
Kosta "Ventana" egg paperweight designed by Mona Morales-Schildt ca. 1960, with internal layer of orange, raspberry pink and yellow glass, concave surface cuts on both sides, and an internal suspended bubble on the center, signed. *Sweden*
Height 3 in; 7.6 cm.
$400-500

Nuutajarvi Notsjo vase designed by Unto Suominen ca. 1964, of tapered cylindrical form in amber glass, and heavy clear glass base with facet cuts around it, signed US Nuutajarvi Notsjo-64. *Finland*
Unto Souminen was a master glassblower for Nuutajarvi Notsjo. During the 1960s, some of his designs were put into production.
Height 8-3/4 in; 22.25 cm.
$250-350

Riihimaen Lasi "Majakka" (lighthouse) vase, designed in 1960 by Aimo Okkolin, in lilac alexandrite glass.
Height 10 in; 25.4 cm.
$800-1000

Opposite:
Kosta "Atlantis" vase designed by Vicke Lindstrand ca. 1958, of bulbous form, internally decorated with amethyst strands resembling a net, and surface cuts resembling fish, signed. *Sweden*
Height 5-1/2 in; 14 cm.
$900-1000

47

Kosta Boda "Moonlanding" series designed by Monica Backstrom in 2000, showing vases and bowls with textured surface with slices removed to reveal layers of color. *Sweden*

Photo courtesy of Kosta

Kosta Boda bowls designed by Kjell Engman in 1988, delicate bubble-like form in blue turning into tan
with diagonally sliced rims. *Sweden*
Diameter 6 in; 15.25 cm
$125-175 each

Unique "Matalikko" (Shallows) bowl designed by Kerttu Nurminen in 1998, disc form with carved surface
of leaves and berries. This piece was executed at the Nuutajarvi Glassworks and was part of the
"Acquatico" exhibition in the Galleria San Nicolo in Venice.

Photo by Timo Kauppila courtesy of iittala

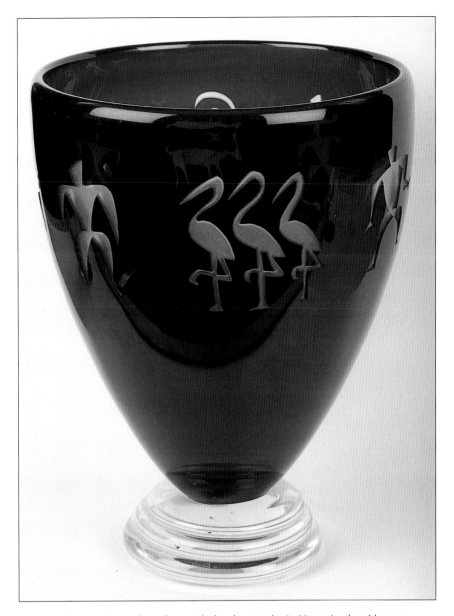

Deep purple cased over clear glass, with deeply carved primitive animal and human forms, sandblasted to create frosted effect on the figures. Signed and numbered, presumed to be Scandinavian.
Height 9-1/2 in; 24.1 cm.

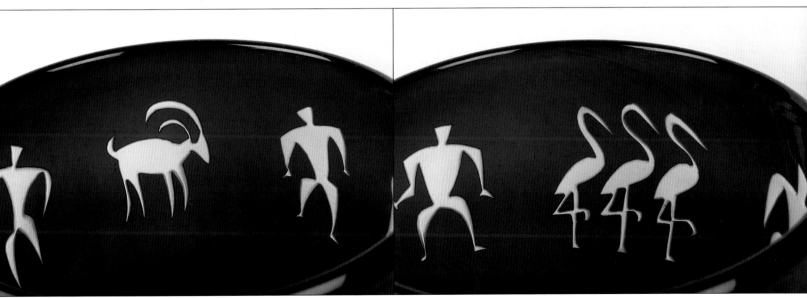

Details.

Chapter 4 • Molded

iittala "Nappi" designed by Markku Salo in 1998; flattened disc shaped candleholders with textured surface. *Finland*
$15-25 each depending on color

Photo by Timo Kauppila courtesy of iittala

Gullaskruf "Randi" opaque blue bowls, designed by Arthur Percy in the mid-1950s, labels. *Sweden* Diameters 3-1/2 and 6-1/2 in; 8.9 and 16.5 cm.
$50-75 each

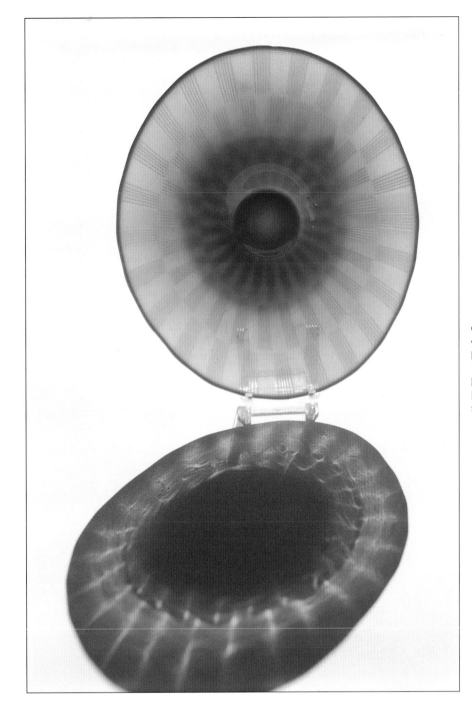

Gullaskruf "Randi" plate in blue with textured surface, designed by Arthur Percy in the mid-1950s, distributed by Raymor, labels. *Sweden*
Diameter 8-3/4 in; 22.25 cm.
$60-80

Gullaskruf red "Randi" bowls, Arthur Percy. *Sweden*
Diameters 3-1/2, 6-1/2 and 9 in; 8.9, 16.5, and 23 cm.
$50-100 each, depending on size

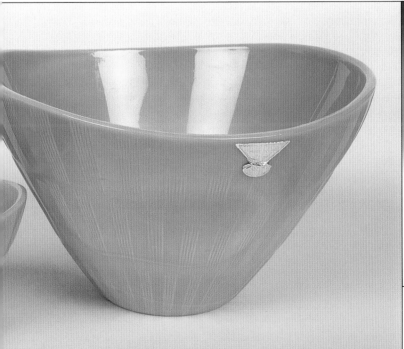

Kumela candleholder bowls in deep amethyst, label. *Finland*
Diameter 6-1/2 in; 16.5 cm.
$30-40 each

Hadeland vase or bowl designed by Willy Johansson, externally ribbed glass and internally decorated with blue, green and amethyst particles, signed. *Norway*
Diameter 6 in; 15.25 cm.
$150-200

Humppila bowl from the "Kasvimaalla" (Vegetable Garden) series designed by Pertti Santalahti in the mid to late 1970s, in the form of a flower with green center and clear petals, signed. *Finland*
Diameter 8 in; 20.3 cm.
$75-100

Riihimaen Lasi bowl in the form of a large blue flower, label. *Finland*
Diameter 11 in; 28 cm.
$60-80

Humppila bowls with honey center and clear rim, designed by Pertti Santalahti in the mid to late 1970s, signed. *Finland*
Diameter 9 in and 13 in; 23 and 33 cm.
$75-150 each, by size

Humppila heavy rock-like bowl, designed by Pertti Santalahti likely in the mid to late 1970s, in amber and clear, signed. *Finland*
Diameter 8-1/2 in; 21.6 cm.
$75-100

Humppila "Revontulet" (Northern Lights) heavy rock-like shallow bowl, designed by Tauno Wirkkala in the early 1970s, in amber and clear, signed. *Finland*
Diameter 12 in; 30.5 cm.
$100-125

Opposite:
Humppila "Revontulet" vase designed by Tauno Wirkkala in the early 1970s, with celery green and clear fingers creating an irregular flared rim, signed. This series of bowls and vases by Tauno Wirkkala is the most recognized production of the Humppila Glassworks. *Finland*
Height 11 in; 28 cm.
$175-225

Humppila "Revontulet" deep bowl designed by Tauno Wirkkala in light and deep amber with thin rock crystal fingers radiating from center. *Finland*
Diameter 12-1/2 in; 31.75 cm.
$100-200

Humppila "Revontulet" deep bowl designed by Tauno Wirkkala, clear and deep amber with thin rock crystal fingers radiating from center. *Finland*
Diameter 9 in; 23 cm.
$75-125

Kumela "Kallio" (rock) vases designed by Kai Blomqvist ca. 1970s, with textured surface like ice blocks or rocks, in amber and amethyst glass, signed. *Finland*
Height 8-1/4 in; 21 cm.
$175-225

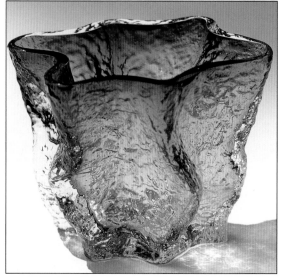

Kumela "Kallio" (rock) vase in celery green, and amethyst glass, vase with similar texture, designed by Kai Blomqvist ca. 1970s, signed. *Finland*
Heights 9 and 6 in; 23 and 15.25 cm.
$125-225 each

Shorter vase in earthy brown.

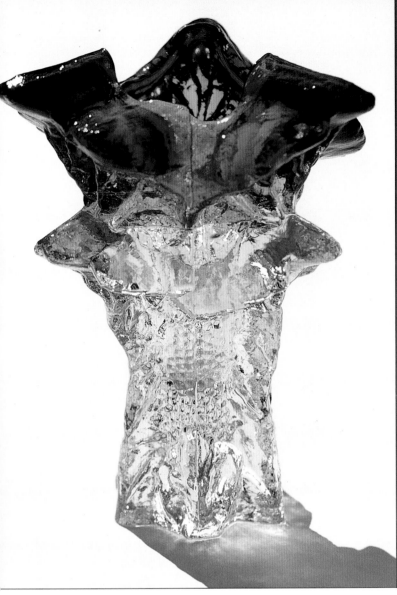

Humppila vase from the "Kasvimaalla" (Vegetable Garden) series designed by Pertti Santalahti in the mid to late 1970s, molded in the form of a vegetable-like plant with lime greens at the top and clear base, signed. *Finland*
Height 8-1/2 in; 21.6 cm.
$100-150

Humppila candleholders from the "Kasvimaalla" (Vegetable Garden) series designed by Pertti Santalahti in the mid to late 1970s, in chunky icy texture and form, both clear, one with deep blue and the other deep green base, signed. *Finland*
Height 10-1/2 in; 26.7 cm.
$75-125 each

Detail.

Riihimaen Lasi off-sided, cased cylindrical vase in acid green with clear base. *Finland* Height 8-1/2 in; 21.6 cm. $70-90

Nuutajarvi Notsjo "Kastehelmi" (dewdrop) candleholder vases, designed by Oiva Toikka in 1964, in intense blue with molded spots. *Finland* Height 6 in; 15.25 cm. $50-75 each in blue

Gotlandshyttan vase in pale green in traditional form with foot and texture. *Sweden* Height 8-1/2 in; 21.6 cm. $70-90

Riihimaen Lasi "Grapponia" square bottle flasks designed by Nanny Still in 1968, in vaseline and moss green glass, with overall prunts in a circle motif. *Finland*
Height 7-1/2 in; 19 cm.
$175-225

Riihimaen Lasi "Aurinko" (sun) bottle vases, designed by Helena Tynell in 1962 and produced from 1964 to 1974, with a sunray motif resembling a sunflower, in vaseline glass, with flat flared rims. These bottles vases are likely one of the most recognized designs ever produced by Riihimaki. *Finland*
Heights 5, 7, and 9 in; 13, 18, and 23 cm.
$100-250 each, by size

Riihimaen Lasi vaseline glass vases under black light. *Finland*

Riihimaen Lasi "Roudella" Vaseline glass vase designed by Tamara Aladin ca. 1970, with squared sides, each with two concentric circles filled with beads. *Finland*
Height 10 in; 25.4 cm.
$200-300

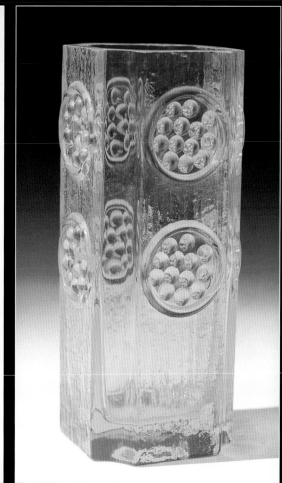

Riihimaen Lasi vaseline glass vase in squared form with two concave sides with texture of solid bubbles or beads, attributed to Tamara Aladin ca. 1970. *Finland*
Height 11 in; 28 cm.
$200-300

Riihimaen Lasi vaseline glass "Rengas" (ring) vase designed by Tamara Aladin, ca. 1972, with squared sides and flared rim, textured with concentric circles. *Finland*
Height 10 in; 25.4 cm.
$200-300

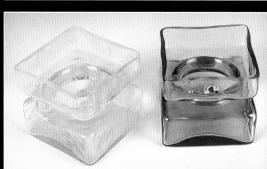

Riihimaen Lasi "Pala" (piece) vases designed by Helena Tynell in 1964 and produced form 1964 to 1976 in vaseline and lilac glass. *Finland*
Height 2.3/4 in; 7 cm.
$75-100 each

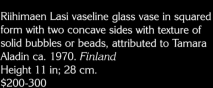

Kumela squared vase in amethyst with geometric symbols on each side, designed by Pentti Sarpaneva in 1970, with patinated lace silver band from Finnish silver and jewelry maker, Turun Hopea. *Finland*
Height 8 in; 20.3 cm.
$150-200

Kumela vase in shades of amber. *Finland*

The silver band has the maker's mark, Finnish silver mark, city mark for Turku, and R7 for 1970. *Finland*

Kumela Pentti Sarpaneva vase in blue with metal mount. *Finland*
Height 5-3/4 in; 14.6 cm.
$100-150

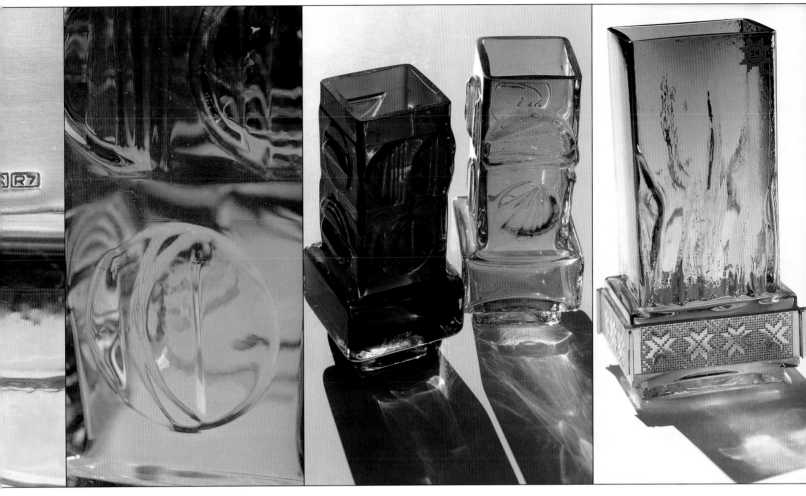

Detail

Newer versions, ca. late 1970s, of Kumela vase designed by Pentti Sarpaneva with more rounded base, no metal band, and no signature. *Finland*
Height 8 in; 20.3 cm.
$70-90

Humppila squared vase with a different pattern, mounted in metal band with hallmark. *Finland*
Height 9 in; 23 cm.
$100-150

Aseda pillow vases in deep blue and light amber, with vertical ribs and ground rims, designed by Bo Borgstrom, ca. late 1960s. *Sweden*
Heights 8 in; 20.3 cm.
$100-125 each

Humppila vases in apple green and honey, vertical crystal texture designed by Tauno Wirkkala, produced from 1972 to 1987, signed. *Finland*
Heights 10 and 6-1/2 in; 25,4 and 16.5 cm.
$125-200 each

Riihimaen Lasi "Locullus" squared vase designed by Nanny Still in 1966, of pale amber glass with a line-dot motif, with blue and white paper label which reads "Made in Finland". There are nine vases in the "Locullus" series, all of them with different molded designs. *Finland*
Height 7-1/2 in; 19 cm.
$150-200

Kumela square vase in clear and blue glass with molded motif on two sides, with label.
Height 7-3/4 in; 19.7 cm.
$125-175

Skruf vase in apple green cased in clear glass, with bubble wrap pattern, possibly designed by Bengt Edenfalk. *Sweden*
$75-100

Riihimaen Lasi "Emma" vase designed by Helena Tynell in 1976, in cherry red cased in clear glass, with label. *Finland*
Height 9 in; 23 cm.
$200-250

Kumela vase of amoeboid abstract form in honey tones, designed by Kai Blomqvist in the early 1970s, signed. *Finland*
Width 7-1/4 in; 18.4 cm.
$150-200

Flygsfors vase designed by Wiktor Berndt in 1960, in mossy green with stylized bird figure, molded in relief and then ground, signed. *Sweden*
Height 5-1/2 in; Length 8 in; 14 and 20.3 cm.
$350-400

Chapter 5 • Hot

Kosta Boda "Galaxy Blue" Artist Collection series designed by Bertil Vallien in 1980. *Sweden*
Photo courtesy of Kosta Boda

Kosta Boda "Galaxy Blue" vase designed by
Bertil Vallien in 1980 from the Artist
Collection (limited production), signed.
Sweden
Height 8-3/4 in; 22.25 cm.
$200-250

Opposite:
Kosta Boda blue rectangular vases with black
and white murrhines, and white irregular pillow
vase with threaded design, both designed by
Bertil Vallien in 1987. *Sweden*
Heights 6-1/2 and 7-1/2 in; 16.5 and 19 cm.
$200-250 each

Nuutajarvi Notsjo unique footed bowl designed by Kaj Franck ca. 1970s, of highly textured, "slush" or "exploded" opaque gray glass, with abstract surface additions of black, clear, and yellow glass.
This technique, referred to as "slush" or "exploded" glass in the literature, was employed by Kaj Franck extensively during the 1970s.

Photo courtesy of iittala

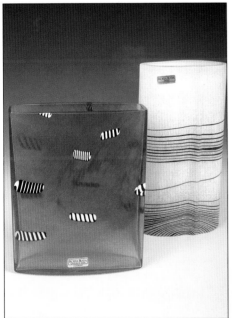

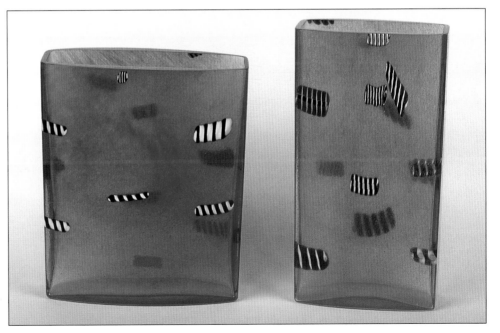

Kosta Boda "Satellite" series designed by Bertil Vallien in 1992. *Sweden*
Photo courtesy of Kosta Boda

Nuutajarvi Notsjo sculpture, "Saarella Palaa II", designed by Oiva Toikka. *Finland*

Detail.

Skruf spun and threaded vases designed by Bengt Edenfalk in the mid- to late 1950s, with applied threading in various heights and shapes, signed. *Sweden*
Heights 8 to 13 in; 20.3 and 33 cm.
$350-700, depending on size

Skruf spun and threaded bowl designed by Bengt Edenfalk in the mid to late 1950s, in amethyst glass with applied threading, signed. A vase from these series of threaded art glass pieces was exhibited in the Corning Glass Museum exhibition of 1959, in conjunction with pieces in the "Thalatta" technique. *Sweden*
Diameter 6 in; 15.25 cm.
$250-300

Skruf spun and threaded vases designed by Bengt Edenfalk in the mid- to late 1950s, with applied threading in various heights and shapes, signed. *Sweden*
Heights 8 to 13 in; 20.3 and 33 cm.
$350-700, depending on size

Sea Glasbruk vase of early company production from the late 1950s or early 1960s, in deep blue-violet glass with frosted bottom half with applied threading. *Sweden*
Height 8 in; 20.3 cm.
$50-75

Johansfors bowl and vase designed by Bengt Orup in vivid blue with applied bands of clear cloud shaped glass, signed. *Sweden*
Bowl diameter 6 in; 15.25 cm.
Vase height 9 in; 23 cm.
$400-500 each

Aseda vase, designed by Bo Borgstrom ca.1960s, in violet with applied clear glass. *Sweden*
Height 10 in; 25.4.cm.
$75-100

Aseda decanters designed by Bo Borgstrom ca. 1960s, in honey and deep blue with applied clear glass blobs and clear stopper. The honey decanter retains the "E and R Golden Crown Sweden" import label, which can often be found in Aseda pieces. The deep blue decanter retains a "made in Sweden" paper label. *Sweden*
Height 9 in; 23 cm.
$100-125 each

Chapter 6 • Spots

Top Left:
Randsfjordglass globular vase designed by Benny Motzfeldt ca. late 1960s, with mottled blues, tans, and green splashes with spots and bubbles, signed. *Norway*
Height 6 in; 15.25 cm.
$300-400

Bottom Left:
Plus Norway bubbly globular vase in honey amber glass. *Norway*
Height 6-3/4 in; 17.1 cm.
$250-350

Top Right:
Randsfjordglass globular vase designed by Benny Motzfeldt ca. late 1960s, in bubbly blues with undersea effect, label. *Norway*
Height 5-1/2 in; 14 cm.
$250-350

Bottom Right:
Lindshammar vase, designed by Gunnar Ander likely in the late 1960s, of olive colored glass, with wide cylindrical body overlapping thin speckled neck, signed. *Sweden*
Height 6 in; 15.25 cm.
$175-225

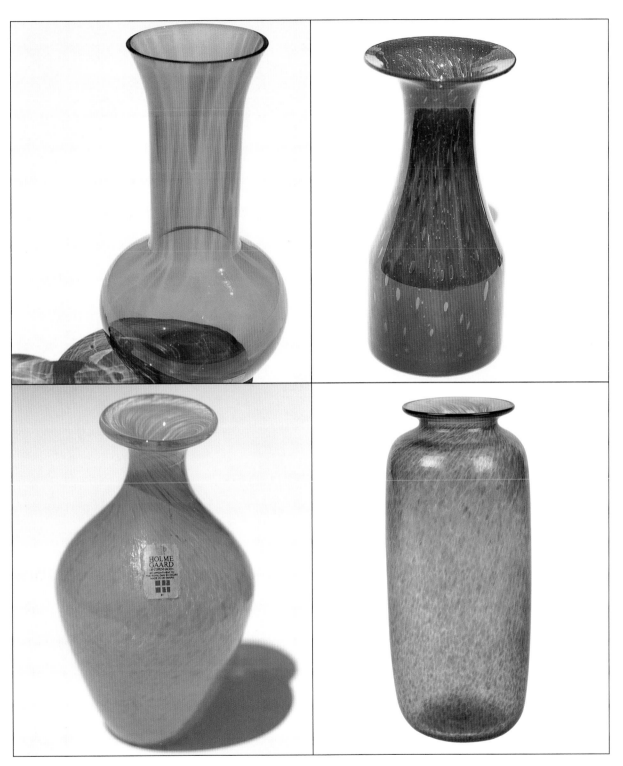

Top Left:
Lindshammar vase designed by Christer Sjogren ca. 1960s, in apricot orange glass mottled with white glass spots, with elongated neck and slightly flared rim. *Sweden*
Height 11 in; 28 cm.
$150-200

Bottom Left:
Holmegaard cased vase in mottled sky blue, label. *Denmark*
Height 5-1/4 in; 13.3 cm.
$100-125

Top Right:
Plus Glasshytte bottle-vase in fiery reds with flared rim. *Norway*
Height 7-1/2 in; 19 cm.
$200-250

Bottom Right:
Pink and lavender mottled vase likely designed by Erik Hoglund, signed Hoglund 1992. Erik Hoglund worked on a freelance basis in the 1980s and 1990s for some glassworks as well as designing exclusive glass pieces for retailers such as Duka, in Sweden. *Sweden*
Height 6-1/4 in; 15.9 cm.
$200-300

Ekenas cylindrical vase designed by John-Orwar Lake, likely in the late 1960s or 1970s, in unusual pinkish lilac glass, signed. *Sweden*
Height 8-3/4 in; 22.25 cm.
$300-400

Randsfjordglass cylindrical cased vase designed by Benny Motzfeldt ca. late 1960s, in blue bubbly glass, label. *Norway*
Height 5-1/2 in; 14 cm.
$250-350

Magnor vase, heavy teal underlay cased in clear glass, with regular netting of bubbles. *Norway*
Height 8-1/4 in; 21 cm.
$150-200

Opposite:
Nuutajarvi Notsjo vases designed by Gunnel Nyman in 1947, in amber and amethyst glass heavily cased in clear glass, with an internal veil of controlled bubbles, signed. *Finland*
Heights 10 and 10-3/4 in; 25.4 and 27.2 cm.
$1000-1200

Kosta "Seaweed" vases designed by Vicke Lindstrand in 1962, heavy clear glass with internal green seaweed decoration, the smaller engraved with fish on both sides, signed. *Sweden*
Heights 8-1/2 and 11 in; 21.6 and 28 cm.
$400-500

Kosta "Seaweed" bowl designed by Vicke Lindstrand in 1962. *Sweden*
Diameter 6-1/2 in; 16.5 cm.
$300-400

Detail.

Top Left:
Randsfjordglass vase designed by Torbjorn Torgersen, stretched globular form with tiny opening, internally decorated with muted purples and pinks. *Norway*
Height 8-3/4 in; 22.25 cm.
$300-400

Bottom:
Kosta Boda Atelier (limited production) "Cassiopeia" series, designed by Anna Ehrner in 1991. *Sweden*
Photo courtesy of Kosta Boda

Top Right:
Kosta Boda "Frutteria" gourd shaped vases, designed by Gunnel Sahlin in 1990 with mottled colored glass, one pink and the other green, signed. *Sweden*
Height 9 in; 23 cm.
$250-300 each

Vase, possibly produced by Lindshammar, in pale blue glass with bubbles, elongated neck and sliced rim. *Sweden*
Height 16-1/2 in; 42 cm.
$100-150

Aseda "Bone" vases in red, amethyst, and honey color glass with elongated necks, irregular lip, and square or teardrop bubble-filled paperweight bases. Interestingly, the "Bone" vase design has been traced to Per Lutken in 1952, although his design did not have internal bubbles in the base. Per Lutken's design was never put into production at Holmegaard, but many companies such as Aseda produced variations of the same form, from the 1950s to the 1970s. *Sweden*
Heights 8 to 10 in; 2.3 to 25.4 cm.
$75-125 each

Kosta "Women at Sea" female form vases designed by Mona Morales-Schildt in 1965, with irregular bubbles and internal linear patterns. *Sweden*

Photo courtesy of Kosta Boda

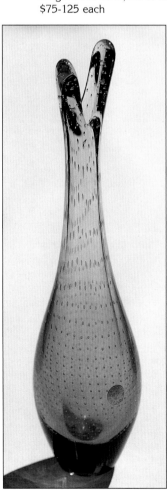

Kastrup vase, ca. 1950s, with regular bubbles in pale blue glass and paperweight base, two irregular pulled lips or "beak." *Denmark*
Height 11-1/2 in; 29.2 cm.
$125-175

Mats Jonasson Maleras "Golden Eye" vases designed by Erika Hoglund, with mottled gold and black, cased in clear glass. *Sweden*

Photo courtesy of Mats Jonasson Maleras

Manthorp ruffled bowl with overall
pattern of irregular spots in purple
plum tones, label. *Sweden*
Diameter 6-1/2 in; 16.5 cm.
$50-75

Hadeland irregular form bowl, designed by Gro Bergslien in
clear glass with clusters of large cobalt blue spots, signed.
Norway
Diameter 11 in; 28 cm.
$150-250

Detail.

Hadeland "Greenland" platters designed by Arne Jon Jutrem in the 1950s, with flat bottoms and straight rims in intense teal filled with bubbles, signed. *Norway*
Diameters 8 and 14 in; 20.3 and 35.6 cm.
$250-400 each, by size

Kumela thick-walled triangular bowl, with 14 internal purple sunrays surrounded by 14 cloudy scallops, each with one large trapped air bubble, designed by Armando Jacobino in the 1960s, signed. *Finland.*
Length 5-1/4 in; 13.3 cm.
$150-175

Detail.

Boda cased footed bowl of mostly blue bubbly glass and large patches of deep amber, designed by Bertil Vallien ca. 1970s, with label. *Sweden*
Diameter 4 in; 10.2
$125-150

Kosta bowl designed by Ann and Goran Warff ca. late 1960s or early 1970s, in deep sea blue with purple accents, signed. *Sweden*
Diameter 8-1/4 in; 21 cm.
$250-300

Ekenas bowl designed by John-Orwar Lake, ca. late 1960s or 1970s, in bubbly rose tones, with heavy clear foot, signed. *Sweden*
Diameter 7 in; 17.8 cm.
$200-250

Bjorkshult bowl in bubbly glass textured with dark spots, label. *Sweden*
Diameter 8 in; 20.3 cm.
$125-150

Bowl of heavy cased red and clear glass with regular bubbles, designed by F.W. Johanson, signed. *Sweden*
Diameter 6-1/2 in; 16.5 cm.
$60-80

Johansfors bowl designed by Bengt Orup likely in the 1960s, in clear glass with tiny blue spots and abstract pattern of blues and browns, signed. *Sweden*
Diameter 5 in; 12.7 cm.
$150-200

Kosta vase designed by Ann and Goran Warff ca. 1960s, in an oblong shape with regular pattern of blue, amethyst, and raspberry flame-like forms cased in clear glass, signed. *Sweden*
Length 4 in; 10.2 cm.
$350-400

Lindshammar "Zorba" bowls designed by Lars Sestervik ca. 1990s, with tapered sides and wide rims, large blue and beige abstract swirling shapes. *Sweden*

Photo courtesy of Lindshammar

Mats Jonasson Maleras "Fragancia" vase designed by Klas-Goran Tinback in 2000, of tapered form, with a marble-like underlay of blue, white and black glass, cased in clear glass. The "Fragancia" series is still in production at Mats Jonasson Maleras today.

Photo courtesy of Mats Jonasson Maleras

Mats Jonasson Maleras "Caribbean Blue" vase designed by Klas-Goran Tinback in 2000, of hourglass form, with a cloud-like pattern of opaque blue, dark amethyst and clear glass. The "Caribbean Blue" series is still in production at Mats Jonasson Maleras today.

Photo courtesy of Mats Jonasson Maleras

Johansfors monumental bowl designed by Bengt Orup likely in the 1960s, infused with overall blue glass particles and large haphazard swirls of blues and browns, signed. *Sweden*
Diameter 11 in; 28 cm.
$400-500

Kosta Boda "Atoll" series of candleholders and bowls, designed by Anna Ehrner in 1992, of simple geometric form in heavy glass and vivid colors, with bold internal airy patterns. *Sweden*

Photo courtesy of Kosta Boda

Kosta Boda "Cancan" series designed by Kjell Engman in 1991, of whimsical form in multitude of colors with heavily textured and abstract patterns. *Sweden*

Photo courtesy of Kosta Boda

Sea Glasbruk "Forever" series of vases and decanters, designed by
Renate Stock in 1999, in textured glass with patterns of two colors spots
- green and blue, orange and blue, yellow and blue. *Sweden*
Photo by Thomas Jeansson, courtesy of Sea Glasbruk

Sea Glasbruk "Duo" double vases, designed by Renate Stock in 1995, in
opaque white with green and blue or purple spots. *Sweden*
Photo by Thomas Jeansson, courtesy of Sea Glasbruk

Sea Glasbruk "Ramelia" series
designed by Bjorn Ramel in 2000, in
either clear frost, blue frost, or yellow
and green spotted. *Sweden*

Photo courtesy of Sea Glasbruk

Nuutajarvi Notsjo goblets designed by Kaj Franck possibly as early as 1965, and produced in the late 1960s to early 1970s, of cylindrical form with free-blown stem and foot, in various color combinations with abstract spotted stems. *Finland*

Photo by Timo Kauppila courtesy of iittala

Nuutajarvi Notsjo goblet vase designed by Kaj Franck ca. 1970s, in lemon
yellow with white bubbly stem and foot, signed. *Finland*
Height 8-1/4 in; 21 cm.
$600-800

Nuutajarvi Notsjo goblet vase designed by Kaj Franck ca. 1970s, in fiery
orange with bubby brown stem and foot and lavender ring, signed. *Finland*
Height 8-1/4 in; 21 cm.
$600-800

Top Left:
Nuutajarvi Notsjo basket bowl designed by Kaj Franck, likely in the 1970s, in shades of green with caramel-like, spotty texture. *Finland*
Photo by Timo Kauppila courtesy of iittala

Bottom Left:
Johansfors cylindrical vase designed by Ingegerd Raman ca. 1970, with folded rim and cluster spray of yellow and green spots, signed. *Sweden*
Height 8 in; 20.3 cm.
$150-250

Top Right:
Nuutajarvi Notsjo "Pantteri" (Panther) vase designed by Saara Hopea in 1955, in clear glass with pattern of air pockets and large green spots. *Finland*
Height 6-1/2 in; 16.5 cm.
$1500-2000
Courtesy of Gordon Harrell

Bottom Right:
iittala "Lido" vase, designed by Tiina Nordstrom in 1985, in clear glass with scattered yellow spots. *Sweden*
Height 7-1/2 in; 19 cm.
$125-175

Ekenas vases designed by John-Orwar Lake ca. late 1960s or 1970s, in bubbly teal and green, signature. *Sweden*
Heights 6 and 8-1/2 in; 15.25 and 21.6 cm.
$200-300 each

Ekenas vase designed by John-Orwar Lake ca. late 1960s or 1970s, in
bubbly pastel bluish and algae green; *Sweden*

Boda vase in bubbly leafy green designed by Erik Hoglund ca. 1960, signed.
Sweden

Heights 6 and 10-3/4 in; 15.25 and 27.3 cm.
$175-225 and $400-600

Ekenas vases designed by John-Orwar Lake ca. late 1960s or 1970s, two
in teal and green, one in bubbly pale bluish and algae green, signature
and label. *Sweden*
Heights 8-3/4 and 6-3/4 in; 22.25 and 17.1 cm.
$200-300 each

Ekenas vase designed by John-Orwar Lake ca. late 1960s or 1970s, in bubbly spotty pale jade green in complex cylindrical shape with flared rim, signed. *Sweden*
Height 6 in; 15.25
$175-225

Ekenas vase designed by John Orwar Lake in transparent bubbly green glass very similar to the style of Erik Hoglund for Boda.
Height 8 in; 20.3 cm.
$200-250

Ekenas vase designed by John-Orwar Lake ca. late 1960s or 1970s, in bubbly pale greenish top portion and bubbly algae green bottom half, signed. *Sweden*
Height 8 in; 20.3 cm.
$300-400

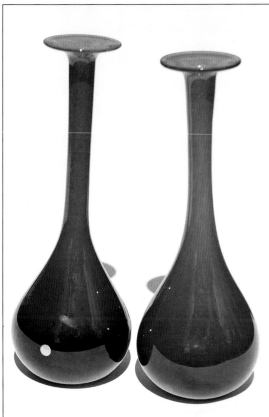

Ekenas vases designed by John-Orwar Lake ca. late 1960s or 1970s, in bubbly spotty red-oranges and indigo blues with varying proportion of intense color, globular base and elongated necks, signed. *Sweden* Heights 10 to 12 in; 25.4 to 30.5 cm. $300-400 each

Ekenas vase designed by John-Orwar Lake ca. late 1960s or 1970s, in bubbly pale greenish and algae green with bulbous base and narrow neck, signed. *Sweden* Height 5-1/2 in; 14 cm. $150-200

Randsfjordglass vase in squared teardrop form in chrome yellow with inky green spots in cluster spray, label. *Norway* Height 9 in; 23 cm.
$300-400

Plus Glasshytte vase designed by Benny Motzfeldt in 1977, in oval form with bubbly steel blue and apricot internal texture, hand incised signature BM 77.
Height 5 in; 12.5 cm.
$350-450

Randsfjordglass vase designed by Hanna Hellum, of globular squared form in thick bubbly opaque yellow and white glass, with splashes of orange and browns, label. *Norway* Height 4-1/4 in; 10.8 cm
$125-175

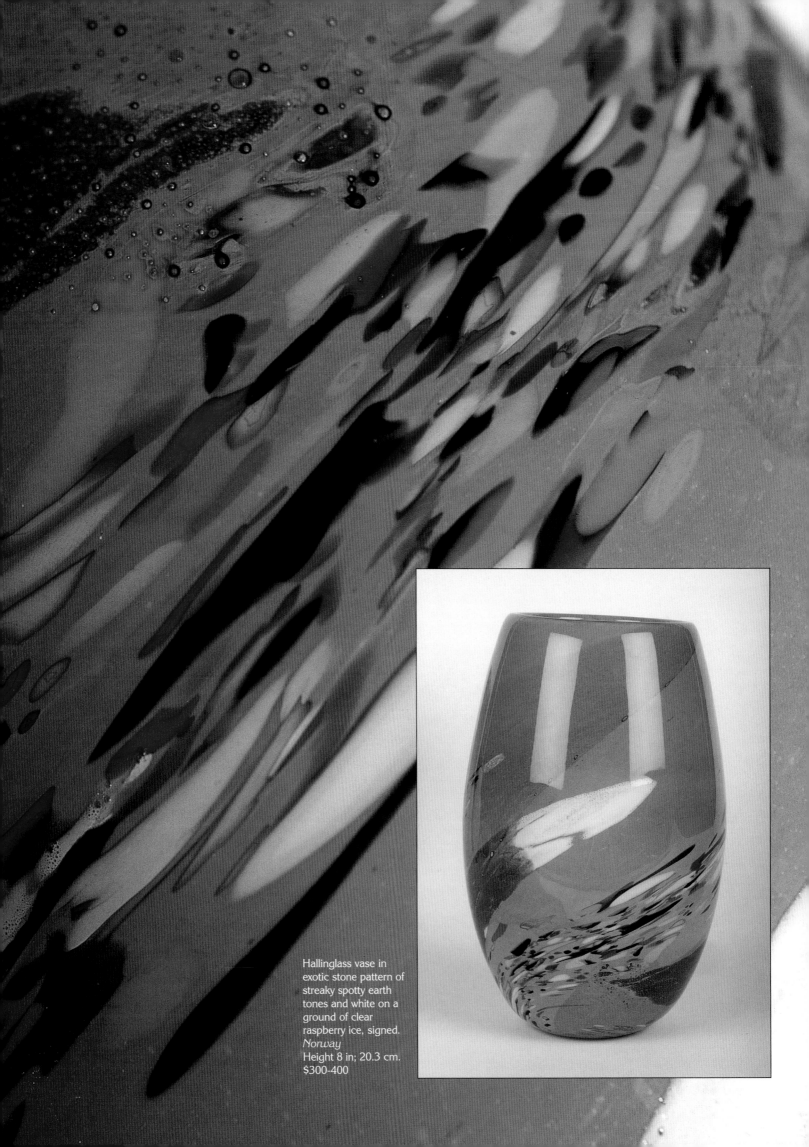

Hallinglass vase in
exotic stone pattern of
streaky spotty earth
tones and white on a
ground of clear
raspberry ice, signed.
Norway
Height 8 in; 20.3 cm.
$300-400

Randsfjordglass cased vases designed by Torbjorn
Torgersen, with indigo blue and lime green swirls and spots
on a ground of clear papaya red, label. *Norway*
Heights 6-1/2 and 7 in; 16.5 and 17.8 cm.
$250-350 each

Randsfjordglass vase and matching bowl designed by Torbjorn Torgersen in same
papaya red color scheme. *Norway*
Diameter 6-1/2 in; 16.5 cm
$250-350

Randsfjordglass low bowl, designed by Torbjorn Torgersen, in similar color scheme with
metallic sparkles and thick crystal exterior. *Norway*
Diameter 6-3/4 in; 17 cm.
$150-250

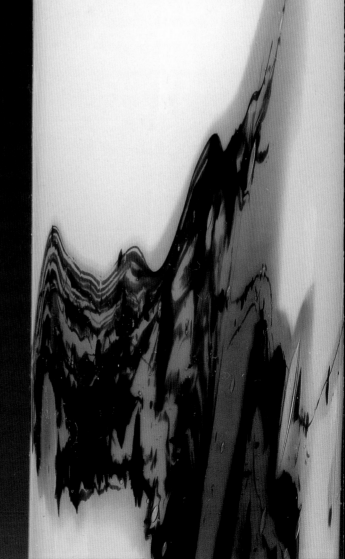

Top:
Holmegaard blown vases designed by Per Lutken and Michael Bang, in opaque white with swirls and spots of fiery reds and oranges, blues, and greens, signed. The cylindrical forms with narrowed and flared necks are from the "Cascade" series, designed by Per Lutken in 1970; the cylindrical form with a globular base and blue and blackish-gray streaks is from the "Atlantis" series, designed by Michael Bang in 1981. *Denmark*
Heights 6-1/2 to 11 in; 16.5 to 28 cm.
$150-250 each

Bottom:
Holmegaard vase and bowl from "Atlantis" series, designed by Michael Bang in 1981.
$150-250 each

Swedish molded vases with similar effect to blown Holmegaard vases, but in muted relatively colorless effect. *Sweden*
Height 7-1/4 in; 18.4 cm.
$40-60 each

Bergdala oblong bowl with large red, white, and blue spots, label. *Sweden*
Length 10 in; 25.4 cm.
$100-150

Holmegaard huge heavy bowl from the "Cascade" series designed by Per Lutken in 1970, in opaque white with multicolored patches, signature and labels. *Denmark*
Diameter 11-1/4 in; 28.6 cm.
$300-400

Dansk International blown vases in opaque lilac with cobalt blue spots and rim, label. *Denmark*
Heights 6 and 9 in; 15.25 and 23 cm.
$100-150 each

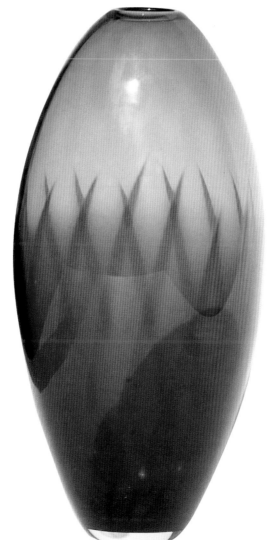

Transjo bulbous cylindrical vase in raspberry magenta flames merging into lilac, signed. *Sweden*
Height 11-1/2 in; 29 cm.
$300-400

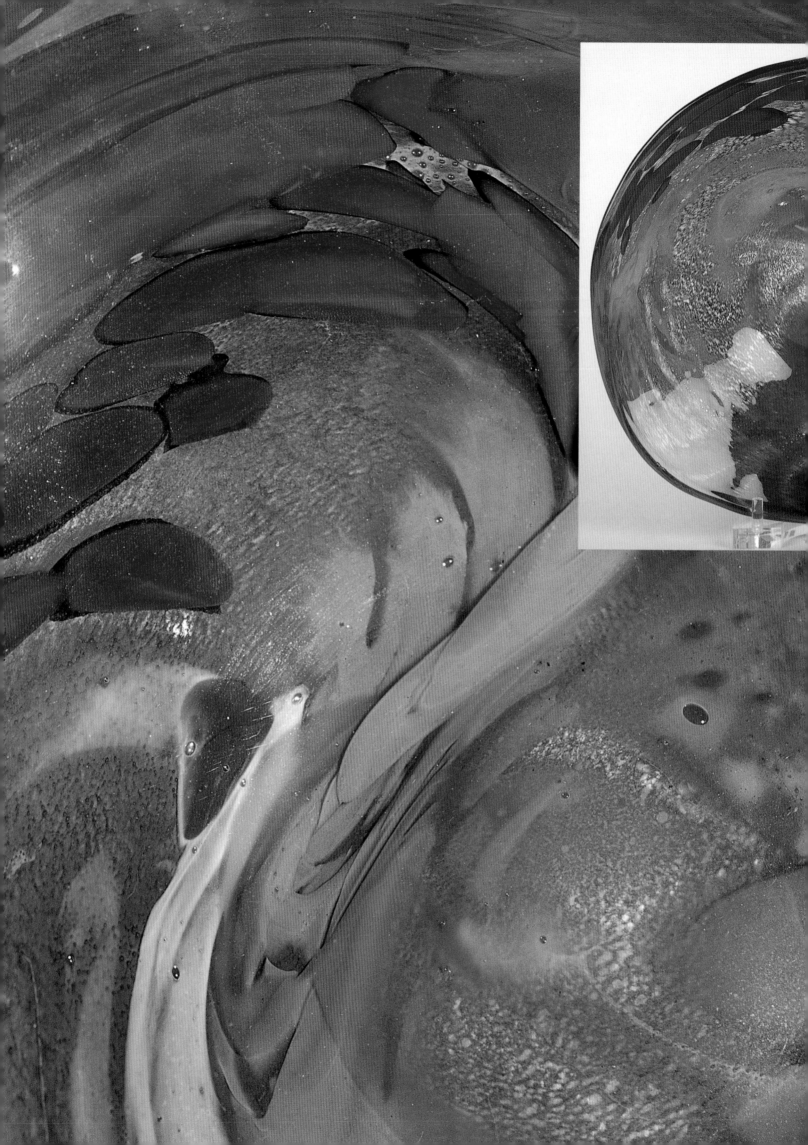

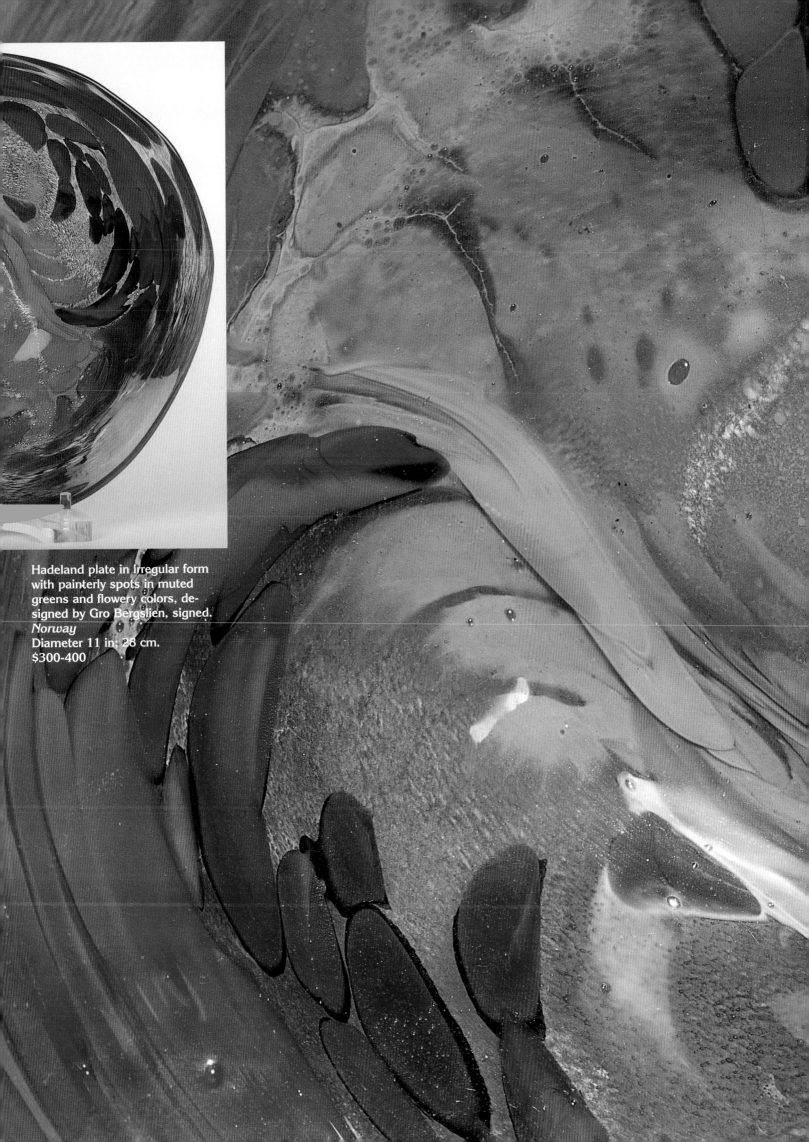

Hadeland plate in Irregular form
with painterly spots in muted
greens and flowery colors, designed by Gro Bergslien, signed.
Norway
Diameter 11 in; 28 cm.
$300-400

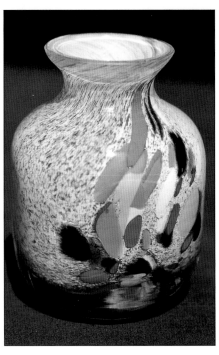

Ekenas huge bowl designed by John-Orwar Lake ca. late 1960s or 1970s, with swirls and spots of forest and meadow colors, signed. Shown with small vase for scale. *Sweden*
Height 8-1/2 in; 21.6 cm.
Diameter 9-1/2 in; 24.1 cm.
$500-700

Randsfjordglass vase designed by Torbjorn Torgersen in mottled opaque white with multicolored spots in clear flowery colors, label. *Norway*
Height 4-1/4 in; 10.8 cm.
$125-150

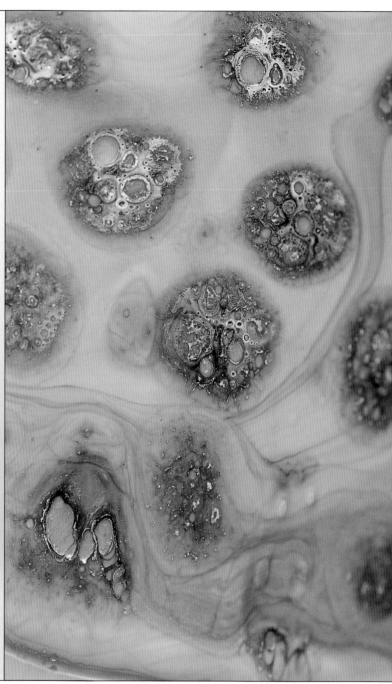

Nuutajarvi Notsjo monumental vase designed by Oiva Toikka, in
earthy tones of khaki with metallic spots, signed. *Finland*
Height 8 in; 20.3 cm.
$1200-1500

Detail.

Randsfjordglass heavy vases designed by Torbjorn Torgersen, in cased opaque white, each internally decorated with spots resembling seeds or beans in shades of brown, labels. *Norway*
Heights 5 and 6 in; 12.7 and 15.25 cm.
$250-350 each

Detail.

Chapter 7 • Stripes

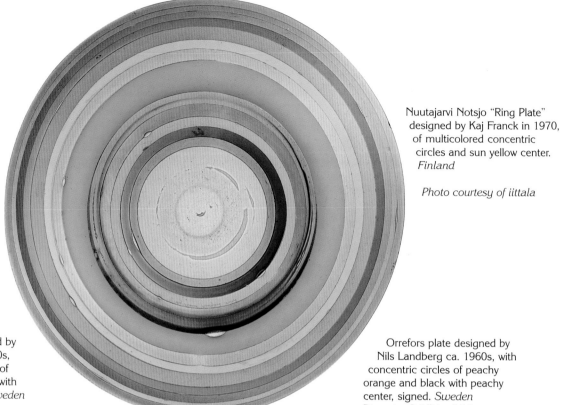

Nuutajarvi Notsjo "Ring Plate" designed by Kaj Franck in 1970, of multicolored concentric circles and sun yellow center. *Finland*

Photo courtesy of iittala

Orrefors plate designed by Nils Landberg ca. 1960s, with concentric circles of cobalt blue and green with blue center, signed. *Sweden* Diameter 9 in; 23 cm. $300-400

Orrefors plate designed by Nils Landberg ca. 1960s, with concentric circles of peachy orange and black with peachy center, signed. *Sweden* Diameter 9-1/2 in; 24.1 $300-400

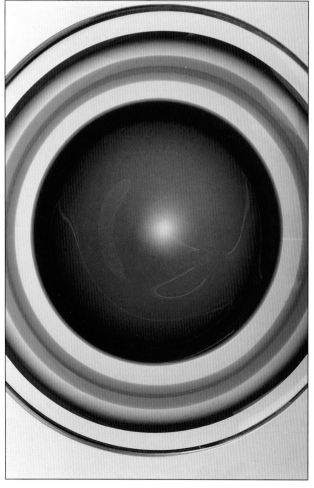

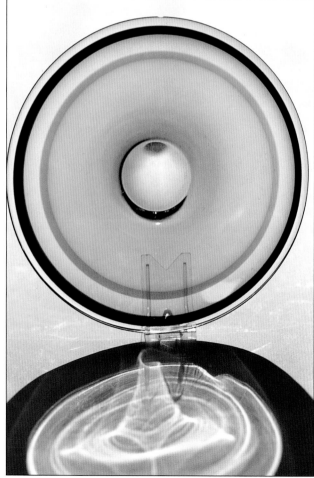

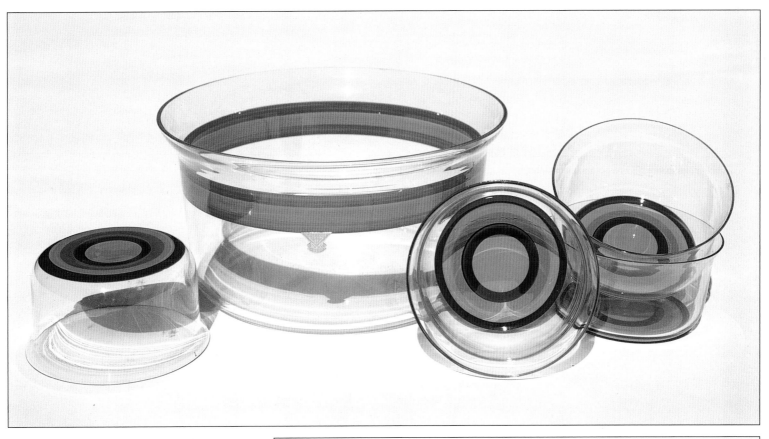

Gullaskruf salad bowl set: large bowl with
enameled orange and red band and small bowls
with concentric circles of blue and green.
Sweden
Diameters 9 and 4-1/2 in; 23 and 11.4 cm.
$150-250 set

Hadeland bowl designed by Arne Jon
Jutrem in 1961 or 1962 in graded olive
green to cobalt blue glass, with molded
lattice pattern and folded rim, signed.
Norway
Diameter 5-3/4 in; 14.6 cm.
$250-300

Kosta bowl in the "Siena" technique designed by Bengt Edenfalk ca. 1986 in opaque white glass with border of linear, pastel colored glass, signed. *Sweden*

The "Siena" technique is one of the treatments Edenfalk created at Kosta during his tenure at the firm. Other techniques he developed at Kosta include "Akvarell," which differs from "Siena" in that he used block-like patches of colored glass suspended in a uniform colored vessel. The "Siena" technique is characterized by a linear design.
Diameter 9-3/4 in; 24.75 cm.
$350-450

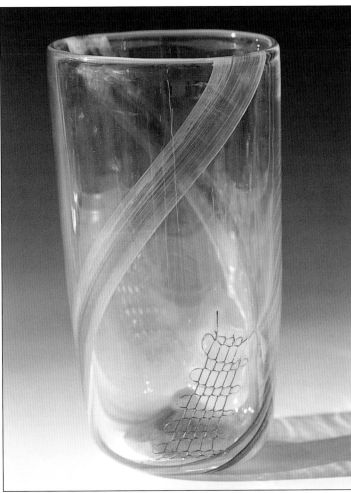

Hallingglass vase with pink and white diagonal stripes and embedded metal screen, signed. *Norway*
Height 8 in; 20.3 cm.
$200-250

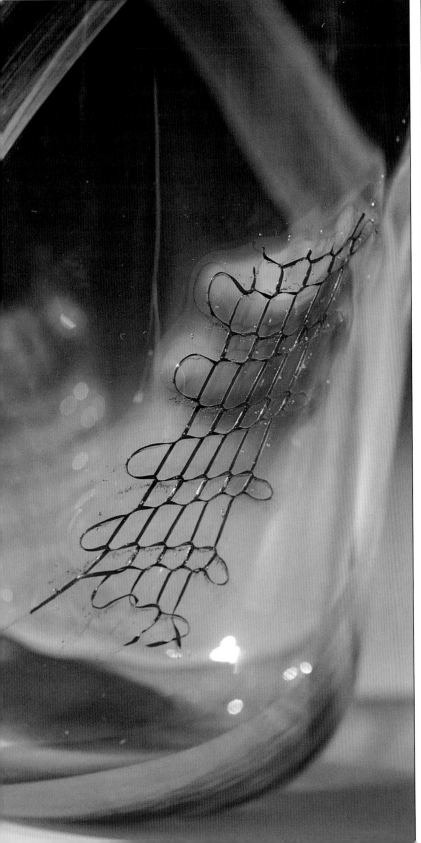

Detail.

Kalmar bowls designed by Tora Pors ca. 1950, in the "Myrica" technique, of heavy clear glass with plum or blue wavy stripes, signed. *Sweden*
Diameters 6 to 8 in; 15.25 to 20.3 cm.
$75-100 each

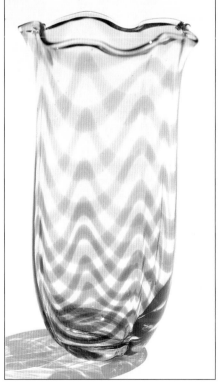

Kalmar vase designed by Tora Pors ca. 1950, in the "Myrica" technique, with ruffled rim and wavy plum stripes. *Sweden*
Height 7-1/4 in; 18.4 cm.
$125-175

Kalmar vase designed by Tora Pors ca. 1950. *Sweden*
Height 4 in; 10 cm.
$100-125

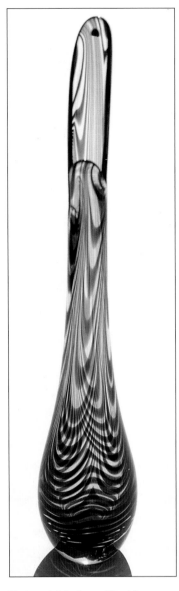

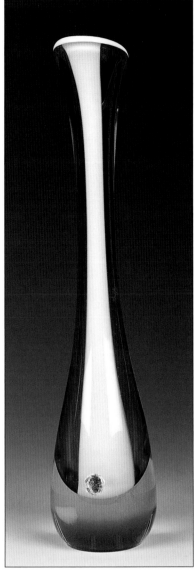

Kastrup tall bulbous "Beak" or "Duckling" vase with elongated neck and uneven rim, plum stripes. *Denmark*
Height 13 in; 33 cm.
$250-300

Kastrup tall bulbous "Beak" or "Duckling" vase with pulled, uneven, beak-like rim, plum stripes. *Denmark*
Height 12 in; 30.5 cm.
$250-300

Sea Glasbruk vase with wide vertical stripes of opaque white and transparent pink, early production ca. 1960s. *Sweden*
Height 13 in; 33 cm.
$125-175

Kalmar heavy melon form vases designed by Tora Pors, ca. 1950, in the "Myrica" technique, with brown, blue, and plum stripes, some signed. *Sweden*
Heights 7-1/2 to 8 in; 19 to 20.3 cm.
$125-175 each

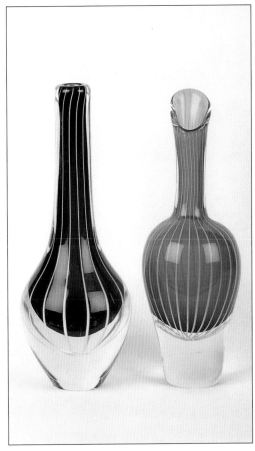

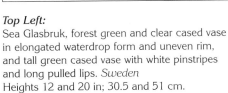

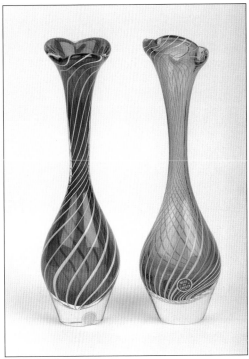

Top Left:
Sea Glasbruk, forest green and clear cased vase in elongated waterdrop form and uneven rim, and tall green cased vase with white pinstripes and long pulled lips. *Sweden*
Heights 12 and 20 in; 30.5 and 51 cm.

Bottom Left:
Sea Glasbruk amethyst pinstripe vase with heavy clear base, and bulbous rim area, early production, ca. 1960. *Sweden*
Height 14 in; 35.5 cm.
$250-350

Heavy cased vases in deep purple, teal green, red, and blue, each with clear paperweight base and opaque white pinstripes. *Sweden*

Many Swedish companies utilized this pinstripe technique during the 1950s and 1960s. Examples by Kosta are easy to identify because those pieces are usually signed and were created by Vicke Lindstrand. Identification of pieces by other companies is more difficult because they were often only labeled, and not signed. Some of the companies that used this technique are Sea Glasbruk (sometimes signed), Glimma Glasbruk, Smalandshyttan, Skruf, and Johansfors.
Heights 9 and 8-3/4 in; 23 and 22.25 cm.
$150-200 each

Kosta vase designed by Vicke Lindstrand around 1950 to 1954, in hot pink with white pinstripes, signed. *Sweden*
Height 3-1/2 in; 9 cm.
$400-500

Orrefors "Ariel" bowl designed by Edvin Ohrstrom, ca. 1937, with air-bubble striped pattern, signed. *Sweden*
Diameter 4-1/2 in; 11.4 cm.
$500-700

Nuutajarvi Notsjo vase designed by Kaj Franck ca. 1950s, of globular form in red glass, with elongated bubble inclusions, signed. *Finland*
Height 3-1/2 in; 8.89 cm.
$350-400

Courtesy of Gordon Harrell

Riihimaki "Vene" vase designed by Nanny Still in 1953, with white filigree pinstripes and cobalt blue glass, cased in clear glass, signed. *Finland*
Kumela vase designed by Armando Jacobino ca. 1960s, with elongated air bubbles, in cobalt blue glass cased in clear glass, signed. *Finland*
Heights 7-1/2 in and 6 in; 19 and 15.25 cm.
$500-700; $300-400

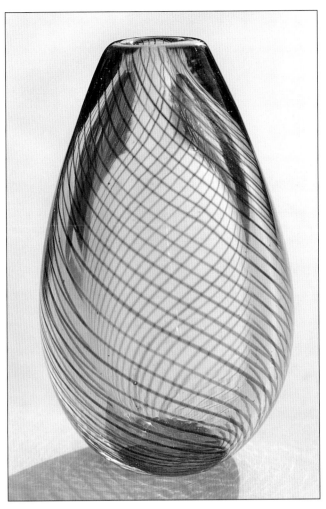

Kosta canoe bowl designed by Vicke Lindstrand ca.1958, with parallel amethyst lines along its body, signed. *Sweden*
Length 12 in; 30.48 cm
$500-600

Hadeland (attributed) teardrop vase with thin diagonal plum stripes. *Norway*
Height 6-1/2 in; 16.5 cm.
$200-300

Orrefors "Graal" vase designed by Edward Hald, made in 1953, purple vertical stripes in thick-walled crystal and paperweight base, signed. *Sweden*
Height 8-1/2 in; 21.6 cm.
$1200-1600

Heavy cylindrical vase tapering to the rim, with purple "stripes" rising from the base, likely Swedish.
Height 12-1/4 in; 31 cm.
$100-125

Nuutajarvi Pro Arte "Palazzo" series designed by Kerttu Nurminen in 1998, various
sizes of vases with thin diagonal filigree stripes in one or two colors. *Finland*

Photo by Timo Kauppila courtesy of iittala

Nuutajarvi Notsjo footed goblet designed by Kaj Franck with thin diagonal filigree stripes in primary colors, signed. *Finland* Height 6-3/4 in; 17.1 cm. $400-500

Unique "Kaislikko" (Rushes) goblet designed by Kerttu Nurminen in 1998, in emerald green glass, with a pattern of segmented lines, giving an appearance of movement. This piece was executed at the Nuutajarvi Glassworks and was part of the "Acquatico" exhibition in the Galleria San Nicolo in Venice. *Finland*

Photo by Timo Kauppila courtesy of iittala

Opposite:
Nuutajarvi Notsjo goblets designed by Kaj Franck and produced from the 1950s to 1970s, each with a colorful array of thin diagonal filigree stripes. *Finland*

Photo by Timo Kauppila courtesy of iittala

Kosta chalice vase designed by Mona Morales-Schildt ca. 1960s, in clear glass with internal bright green lines, signed. *Sweden* Height 9 in; 22.9 cm $600-700

Nuutajarvi Notsjo "Maalaisfiligraani" (Rustic Filigree) stemware designed by
Heikki Orvola in 1972 in feathered opalescent glass.
Photo by Timo Kauppila courtesy of iittala

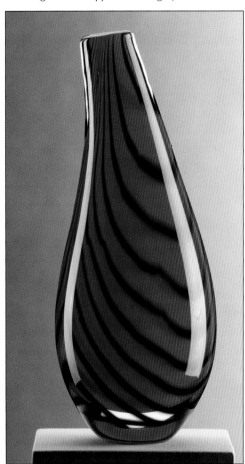

Glimma Glasbruk cased
bulbous vase with narrow neck
in opaque sun yellow with thin
black pinstripes and a clear
foot. *Sweden*
Height 11 in; 28 cm.
$75-100

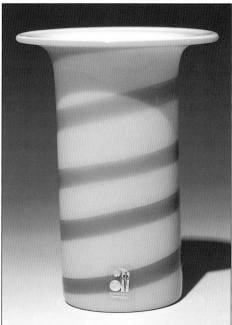

Alsterfors cased cylindrical vase designed by P. O.
Strom ca. late 1960s, with flared rim, in lemon
yellow with wide diagonal green stripes. *Sweden*
Height 5 in; 12.7 cm.
$125-150

Mats Jonasson Maleras "Navarra" vase designed by
Klas-Goran Tinback in 2000, of droplet form, with
a combed pattern of red and black opaque glass.
The "Navarra" series is still in production at Mats
Jonasson Maleras today.

Photo courtesy of Mats Jonasson Maleras

Nuutajarvi Notsjo "Filigraanipulloja" (Filigree Bottles) bottle flasks designed by Kaj Franck, with diagonal, curving and layered filigree stripes in color schemes of pinks, reds and primaries. This example likely dates to the 1970s, although Franck used the filigree technique from the 1950s to the 1970s. *Finland*

Photo by Timo Kauppila courtesy of iittala

Dansk International globular vases with long necks, opaque sky blue with thin diagonal blue and tan stripes, ca. 1970s.
Heights 6 and 8-1/2 in; 15.25 and 21.6 cm.
$75-100 each

Dansk International globular vases in white and teal, each with thin swirling diagonal stripes. Height 5-1/2 and 7-1/2 in; 14 and 19 cm.
$75-100 each

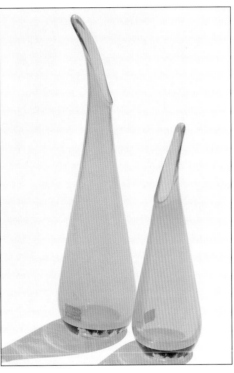

Left and Above:
Gullaskruf tapered cylindrical vases in opalescent canary yellow, irregular lips for free blown sculptural effect. *Sweden*
Heights 8-1/4 and 11-1/4 in; 21 and 28.5 cm.
$125-175 each

Lindshammar vases designed by Gunnar Ander ca. late 1950s, in canary yellow droplet form with asymmetrical pulled rim, label. *Sweden*
Heights 8-1/2 and 12 in; 21.6 and 30.5 cm.
$125-175 each

Glass water droplet mounted in Danish sterling band with three petal-form legs with teal enamel, mount signed. *Denmark*
Height 8-1/2 in; 21.6 cm.
$150-200

Aseda cased vases
designed by Bo
Borgstrom ca. 1960s,
with hot pulled irregular
rims, in amber, moss
green, ocean blue, and
cherry red. *Sweden*
Heights 13 to 16 in; 33
to 4.6 cm.
$75-150 each, by size
and color

Aseda cased
cylindrical bottle
vases designed by Bo
Borgstrom ca. 1960s,
with ground bottoms
and pulled rims, in
same colors as
bulbous vases.
Sweden
Height of tallest 17 in;
43 cm.
$150-200 each

Cased, elongated bone vases, designed by Paul Kedelv, with heavy bases and irregular pulled rims: amethyst and hot pink, pale celery green, and dark purple and emerald green, signed. The first two are from the "Coquille" series designed at Flygsfors, while the third is a "Harlequin" vase designed at Reijmyre in 1958. *Sweden* Heights 13, 15, and 19 in; 33, 38, and 48 cm. $300-500 each

The "Coquille" range is likely the most well-known and commercially successful production of the Flygsfors factory. In French, "coquille" means "shell", and these sea marvels served Paul Kedelv as inspiration for these forms. The "Coquille" range was first introduced in 1952, and production continued until the mid-1960s. Most pieces are signed with the name of the factory, the range ("Coquille"), and the year of production. Some pieces can be found unsigned, and some have a small signature or mark resembling the letters "Sa".

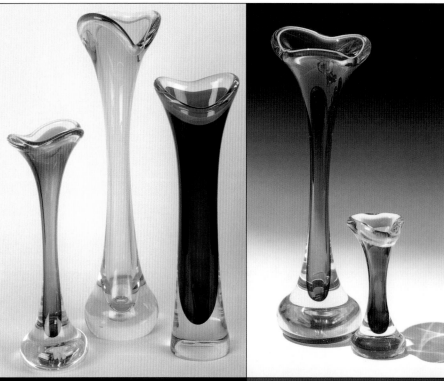

Flygsfors "Coquille" cased elongated vases, designed by Paul Kedelv, in blues, purples, and hot pink, signed. *Sweden* Heights 13 and 5-1/2 in; 33 and 14 cm. $300-350 large; 150-200 small

Coquille sculptural cased floriform bowl, designed by Paul Kedelv, in forest green and white, signed; with Aseda opaque white elongated vase, designed by Bo Borgstrom, ca. late 1960s, similar style as Flygsfors. *Sweden* Diameter 6 in; 15 cm. Height 11 in; 28 cm. $125-150; $70-90

Flygsfors "Coquille" elongated cased vases in leaf green and opaque dark purple, signed. *Sweden* Height 13-1/2 and 18 in; 34 and 46 cm. $300-500 each

Flygsfors "Coquille" cased vase in exaggerated jack-in-the-pulpit form, of dark opaque purple and white, signed. *Sweden*
Height 13 in; 33 cm.
$400-500

Kumela open water droplet form vase by
Armando Jacobino ca. 1960s, in leaf green
and clear, with internal gauze-like layer,
signed. *Finland*
Height 5-1/4; 13.3 cm.
$125-175

RYD and Reijmyre purple and clear cased sculptural bowls.
The small Reijmyre bowl is by Paul Kedelv, designed in
1958, signed. *Sweden*
Length small 5-1/4; 13.3 cm.
$75-125 each

Center:
Flygsfors "Coquille" cased bowls in organic
pulled forms in orange and blue, signature
and label. *Sweden*
Lengths 5-1/2 and 6 in; 14 and 15.25 cm.
$75-150 each

Bottom:
Afors cased sculptural bowls in hot pink and
lime. The hot pink is signed Afors 2007
Rubin, and the green one was designed by
Ernest Gordon, signed. *Sweden*
Length 4-1/2 in; 11.4 cm.
$75-100 each

Flygsfors "Coquille" triangular bowl in violet and hot
pink, signed. *Sweden*
Length 11-1/2 in; 29.2 cm.
$300-400

Flygsfors "Coquille" basket-form bowl in violet and hot
pink, signed. *Sweden*
Height 9-1/2 in; 24.1 cm.
$300-400

Ryd oblong cased bowl in avocado green, label. *Sweden*
Length 8 in; 20.3 cm.
$75-125

Flygsfors three-sided cased bowls in melon and
chartreuse, signed. *Sweden*
Length 7-3/4 in; 19.7 cm.
$175-25 each

Kosta cased bowl, designed by Vicke Lindstrand in 1957, in inky teal blue and clear, signed and engraved "to the Walkers Canadian Embassy Stockholm 1957". *Sweden*
Length 12-1/2 in; 31.75 cm.
$300-400

Ryd oblong cased bowl in deep aqua blue, label. *Sweden*
Length 8 in; 20.3 cm.
$75-125

Flygsfors "Coquille" cased oblong bowls in royal blue, red-orange, and orange, signed.
Lengths 4 to 14 in; 10.2 to 35.6 cm.
$400-600 large bowl

Flygsfors "Coquille" bowl designed by Paul Kedelv in raspberry pink cased in opaque white glass and Sea Glasbruk amethyst glass bowl with opaque glass edging, 1960s production, both signed. *Sweden*
Lengths 6 and 12 in; 15.25 and 30.5 cm.
$75-100 Sea; $250-350 Flygsfors

Flygsfors "Coquille" cased long bowls, designed by Paul Kedelv, with curled ends with opaque white exteriors and hot pink or emerald green interiors, signed. *Sweden*
Average length 12 in; 30.5 cm.
$250-350 each

Flygsfors "Coquille" cased long bowls, designed by Paul Kedelv, with curled ends with opaque white exteriors and hot pink or emerald green interiors, signed. *Sweden*
Average length 12 in; 30.5 cm.
$250-350 each

Randsfjordglass emerald green vase by Torbjorn Torgersen and cased long bowl with turned up ends and heavily indented bottom, labels. *Norway*
Height 8-1/2 in; 21.6 cm.
Diameter 12-1/2 in; 31.75 cm.
$250-350 each

Flygsfors "Fantasia" cased non-vases from the "Coquille" range, designed by Paul Kedelv with four long pulled fingers or tentacles, in raspberry, red-orange, and gray, signed. *Sweden*
Heights 9 and 18 in; 23 and 46 cm.
$250-350 small; $600-800 large

Flygsfors, different version of non-vase by Paul Kedelv, with two pulled sides in hot pink and green, signed. *Sweden*
Height 12 in; 30.5 cm.
$400-600

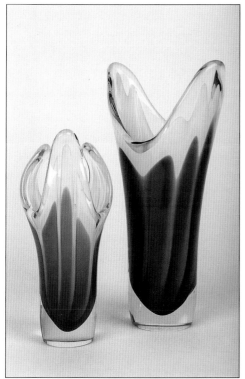

Flygsfors "Coquille" cased non-vase, designed by
Paul Kedelv with three pulled bent fingers in royal
blue and white, signed, and dated 1956. *Sweden*
Height 7-1/2 and 9-1/2 in; 19 and 24.1 cm.
$200-300 each

Flygsfors "Coquille" cased non-vases, designed by Paul Kedelv with two pulled sides, one with fingers,
one in royal blue, the other hot pink with green, signed. *Sweden*
Heights 9-1/4 and 10-3/4 in; 23.5 and 27.3 cm.
$300-400 each

Details.

Left:
Flygsfors "Coquille"
cased manta ray bowls,
designed by Paul Kedelv,
in dark plum and white
in the form of rays with
swishing tails, signed,
dated 1959. *Sweden*
Lengths 8-1/2 and 13 in;
21.6 and 33 cm.
$200-250; $400-500

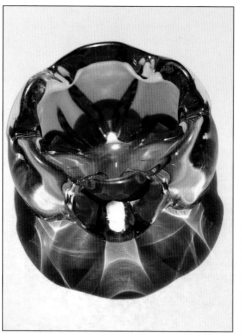

Sea Glasbruk floriform bowl with three petals, in light plum, early 1960s production, signed. *Sweden*
Length 6-3/4 in; 17.1 cm.
$70-90

Afors heavy floriform bowl in rose pink, signed-Afors Bosse Rubin ca. 1950s. *Sweden*
Diameter 4-1/2 in; 11.4 cm.
$100-150

Holmegaard bowl designed by Per Lutken ca. 1955, three-sided in plum, signed. *Denmark*
Length 4 in; 10.2 cm.
$80-100

Kosta floriform bowl in lavender, likely designed by Elis Bergh before the 1950s and later produced in the 1970s, signed. *Sweden*
Diameter 13-1/2 in; 34.3 cm.
$250-350

Kumela flying saucer-shape vase designed by Armando Jacobino in amethyst with elongated bubble inclusions and clear glass ring, ca. 1960s, signed. *Finland*
Diameter 6-1/4 in; 16 cm.
$400-500

Courtesy of Gordon Harrell

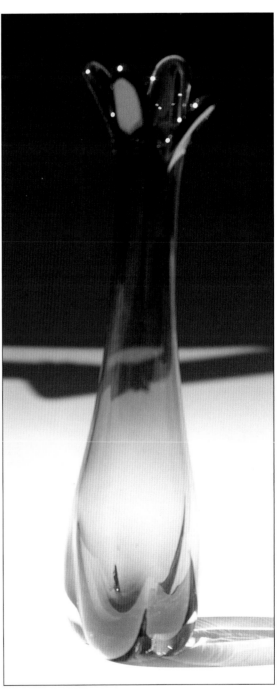

Holmegaard vases designed by Per Lutken ca.1955, three-lobed melon form in plum, signed. *Denmark*
Heights 7-1/4 and 10 in; 18.4 and 25.4 cm.
$250-350 each

Holmegaard vase attributed Per Lutken, elongated with four pulled fingers at rim, in plum. *Denmark*
Height 15 in; 38 cm.
$200-300

Riihimaen Lasi magenta vase designed by Aimo Okkolin ca. 1960S, with bulbous center and tapered top and base, signed. *Finland*
Height 4-3/4 in; 12 cm.
$175-250

Riihimaen Lasi "Meripihka" vase designed by Nanny Still in 1953 with biomorphic form, in deep honey glass and overall sand-blasted and satin texture, signed. *Finland*
Height 3-1/4 in; 8.25 cm.
$300-400

Holmegaard bubble flower arranger vases, designed by Michael Bang in 1973, in leaf green with randomly placed holes, signed and label. *Denmark*
Heights 3, 5-1/2, and 7-1/2 in; 7.6, 14, and 19 cm.
$100-300 each, green, by size

Opposite: Holmegaard vase from the "Cascade" series, designed by Per Lutken in 1970, in heavy irregular sculptural fruit form, opaque white with splashes of clear color, signed. *Denmark*
Height 9 in; 23 cm. Width 11 in; 28 cm.
$500-700

Kosta footed bowl designed by Mona Morales-Schildt ca. 1960s, with an underlay of amber glass, heavily cased on clear glass, signed. *Sweden*
Diameter 6-1/2 in; 16.51 cm
$400-500

Kosta paperweight designed by Ann and Goran Warff ca. early 1970s, with a suspended bubble amongst a cobalt glass flower, signed. *Sweden*
Height 3 in; 7.6 cm.
$175-225

iittala "Aalto" vases and low bowl, designed by Alvar Aalto in 1936, shown in clear, opaque white, and indigo. *Finland*

Photo courtesy of iittala

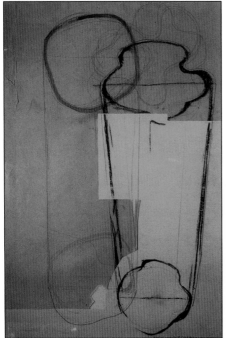

Photograph represents one of the sketches in the series titled "Eskimo Woman's Leather Breeches," with which Aalto won the competition at the Karhula-iittala Glassworks in 1936. The most popular vase in the collection was named "Savoy," and since 1970 was renamed "Aalto" in honor of the designer. This line is still in production at iittala today.

Photo courtesy of iittala

Kosta Boda "Zoom" series, designed by Goran Warff in 1999, in combinations of cobalt blue, clear, and red with large bubble in weighted base. *Sweden*

Photo courtesy of Kosta Boda

Riihimaen Lasi mold-blown "Fantasma" vase in tangerine orange designed by Nanny Still, 1968-1971. *Finland*
Shown with Ingridglass (Germany) vase in similar form, in purple.
Height 11 in; 28 cm.
$250-350

Riihimaen Lasi molded sculptural "Kasperi" vases, designed by Erkkitapio Siiroinen in 1970, with giant flower forms and flat rims, in emerald green and cherry red. *Finland*
Heights 11 and 11-1/2 in; 28 and 29.2 cm.
$250-350 each

Riihimaen Lasi "Pajazzo" (clown) vase with four exaggerated symmetrical red and four vaseline yellow bubbles, flat rim, designed by Nanny Still and produced from 1971-1974. *Finland*
Height 7-1/4; 18.4 cm.
$400-500

Plus Norway bottle vase in rose pink with bubble top and four-sided body, signed. *Norway*
Height 9-1/2 in; 24.1 cm.
$150-200

Hadeland asymmetrical cartoon-form double-bubble vase in cherry red with frosted finish and long neck, designed by Maud Gjeruldsen Bugge in 1991, signed. *Norway*
Height 11-1/2 in; 29.2 cm.
$200-300

Nuutajarvi Notsjo lobed vase designed by Kaj
Franck ca. 1953, in amber cased in clear glass,
signed. *Finland*
Height 4 in; 10.2 cm.
$400-500

Gullaskruf water drop vase, designed in 1989, heavy cased crystal with sea
blues, signed. *Sweden*
Height 9-1/2 in; 24.1 cm.
$300-400

Mats Jonasson Maleras "La Sueca" vase in blues and
greens cased in heavy crystal with thorn-like extensions,
designed by Erika Hoglund. *Sweden*
The "La Sueca" series is still in production at Mats
Jonasson Maleras today.

Photo courtesy of Mats Jonasson Maleras

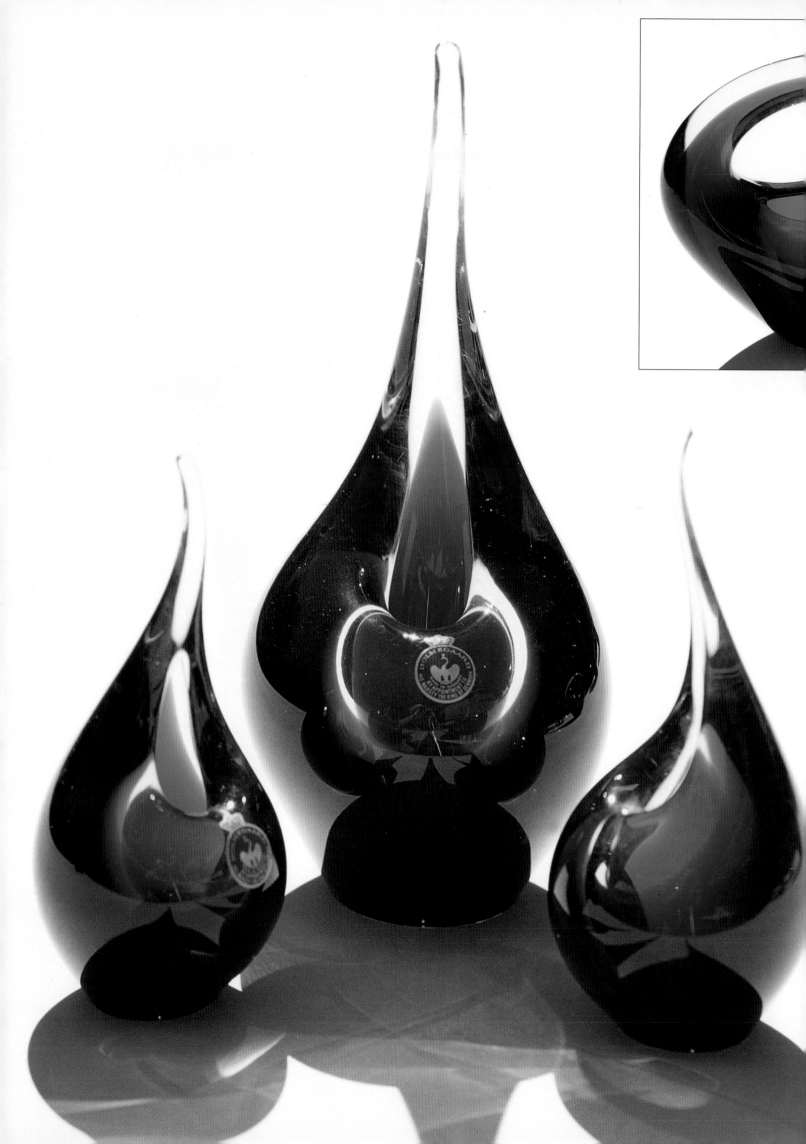

Holmegaard "Abstraction" vessel, designed by Per Lutken
in 1956, of circular form, with underlay of emerald green,
cased in clear glass, signed. *Denmark*
Height 5-1/2 in; 14 cm.
$400-500

iittala "Gilda" abstract, geometrically composed vessel, supported by blue
and tan legs, designed by Heikki Orvola in 1996, executed for the Venezia
Aperto Vetro exposition, the first biennial intended only for art glass. *Finland*

Photo by Timo Kauppila, courtesy of iittala

iittala "Pola Negri" abstract teal vessel and supporting structure in textured
blues and pink, designed by Heikki Orvola. *Finland*

Photo by Timo Kauppila, courtesy of iittala

Left:
Holmegaard water-drop orchid non-vases from the "Abstraction" series, designed by Per Lutken in 1956, in
heavy clear and emerald green glass with depression on one side and thin pulled water top, signed. *Denmark*
Heights 6 and 9-3/4 in; 15.25 and 24.75 cm.
$200-300; $400-500

Chapter 9 • Figural

Detail.

Orrefors "Fishgraal" vase, designed by Edward
Hald in 1936 and first produced in 1938, of
heavy globular form, with green sea flora and
swimming fish, signed. *Sweden*
Height 5 in; 12.7 cm.
$1200-1500

Johansfors cylindrical vase designed by Ingegerd Raman ca. 1970, in mottled pinkish glass with stylized wings in downward movement, signed. *Sweden*
Height 7-3/4 in; 19.5 cm
$300-400

Detail.

Johansfors cylindrical vase designed by Ingegerd Raman ca. 1970, with mottled wheat color background and stylized teal blue bird, signed. *Sweden*
Height 11-1/4 in; 28.6 cm.
$600-800

"Bagno di Bora-Aqua Alta," unique plate designed by Kerttu Nurminen, executed at Nuutajarvi, in browns and blues with a stylized figure of a woman bathing. This piece was presented the Venezia Aperto Vetro exposition, the first biennial intended only for art glass. *Finland*

Photo by Timo Kauppila courtesy of iittala

Kosta Boda unique vase designed by Ulrica Hydman-Vallien in 1999, with enamel painted faces and fish in earth tones, signed. *Sweden*

Photo courtesy of Kosta Boda

Opposite top:
Kosta Boda "Tulipa" series designed by Ulrica Hydman-Vallien in 1992, with primary colored tulip motif on clear glass. *Sweden*

Photo courtesy of Kosta Boda

Opposite bottom:
"Inkivaaripurkki" or "Ginger Jar", a unique design by Heikki Orvola in 1982 executed at Nuutajarvi, consisting of a mold blown jar, sandblasted and etched, with gold leaf pattern. *Finland*

Photo by Gero Mylius courtesy of iittala

Kosta Boda "October" and "May" vases designed by Kjell Engman in 1982 and 1986 respectively, with fired enamel impressionistic scenes with trees, signed. The "October" vase has the Boda signature due to its earlier production. *Sweden*
Heights 8-1/4 and 6-3/4 in; 21 and 17.1 cm.
$225-325 each

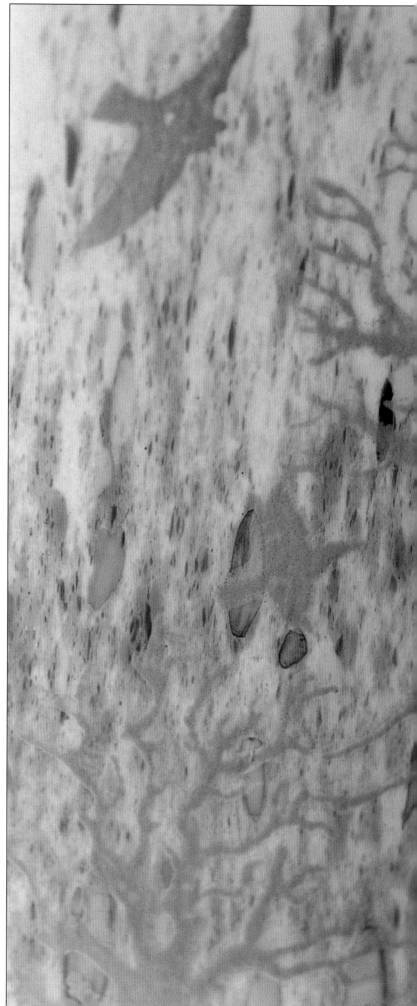

Detail.

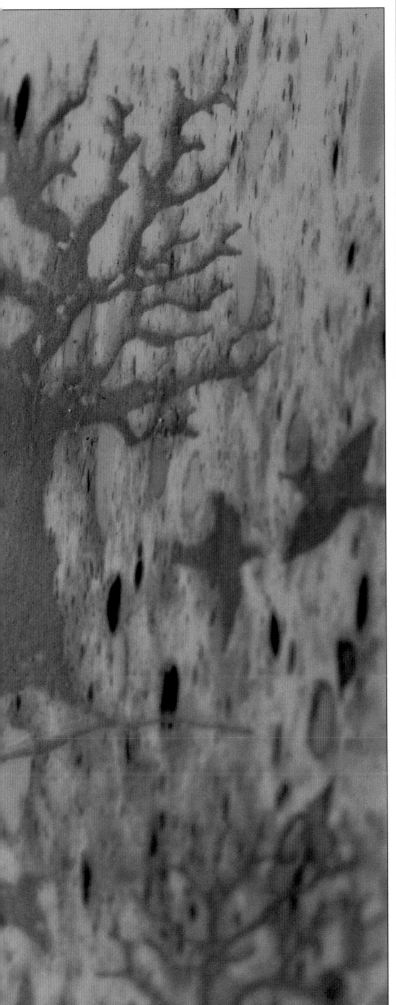

Top:
Lindshammar "Slanda" series designed by Catharina Aselius-Lidbeck in the late 1970s, with painted dragonfly motif. *Sweden*

Photo courtesy of Lindshammar

Bottom:
Boda "November" bowl designed by Kjell Engman in 1982, with fire enameled impressionistic scene with birds, signed. *Sweden*
Diameter 4-1/2 in; 11.4 cm.
$150-200

Boda "Eggs" designed by Monica Backstrom in the 1970s, with naturalistic mottled surface resembling real eggs. *Sweden*

Photo courtesy of Kosta Boda

Boda "Mushrooms" with label, designed by Monica Backstrom in the 1970s.
Sweden
Heights 4-1/2 and 6 in; 11.4 and 15.25 cm.
$100-150; $200-250

Boda "Mushrooms" designed by Monica Backstrom in the 1970s, with naturalistic mottled surface resembling real mushrooms. *Sweden*
Photo courtesy of Kosta Boda

Aseda mushrooms with yellow and orange stems and mottled tops, label. *Sweden*
Height 6-1/2 in; 16.5 cm.
$100-150 each

Aseda mushrooms designed by Bo Borgstrom ca. 1960s, with green stems and spotted tops. *Sweden*
Heights 3-3/4 to 4-1/4 in; 9.5 to 10.8 cm.
$75-100 each

Aseda mushrooms with clear stems and various colored tops with complementary spots. *Sweden*
Height 4-1/2 to 6 in; 11.4 to 15.25 cm.
$75-100 each

Pukeberg knife or cardholders in red-orange.
Sweden
Length 1-3/4 in; 4.5 cm.
$10-15 each

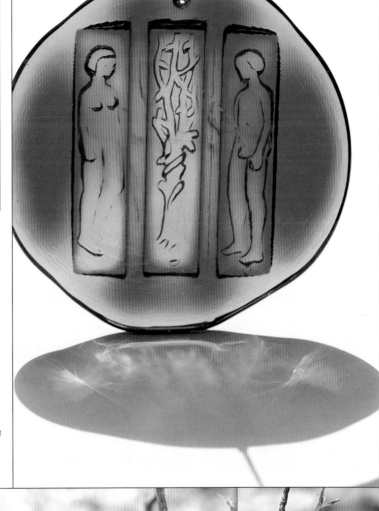

Ekenas suncatchers, with
nude figures representing
Adam and Eve and the
garden in fiery orange and
aqua blue, signed. *Sweden*
Diameters 8-1/4 and 7-1/4
in; 21 and 18.4 cm.
$125-175 each

Boda "People" decanter bottles H/287 and H/288, designed by Erik Hoglund in the late 1950s, one of his most classic and popular designs, two women in bubbly green glass, signed. *Sweden* Height 11-1/4 and 7-3/4 in; 28.5 and 19.5 cm
$200-300; $300-400

Boda 'People" decanter bottles designed by Erik Hoglund in the late 1950s; H/287 woman and H/326 man in brown bubbly glass, signed. *Sweden* Heights 7-1/4 and 9-1/4 in; 18.4 and 23.5 cm.
$200-300; $350-450

Short brown Boda H/327decanter by Erik Hoglund, signed. *Sweden* .
Height 8-1/4 in; 21 cm.
$200-250

Kosta Boda "Precious Cargo" designed by Bertil Vallien in 1986, sand-casted glass sculpture internally decorated, with a fisherman in his boat and the catch of the day. *Sweden*

Photo courtesy of Kosta Boda

Kosta Boda unique sculpture designed by Kjell Engman, white half-globe lamp with cobalt grotesque figures sitting on the edge. *Sweden*

Photo courtesy of Kosta Boda

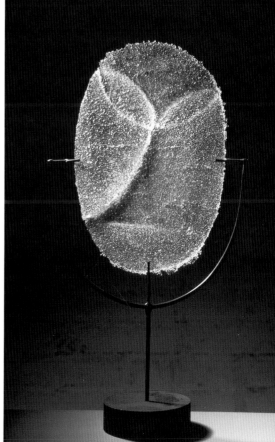

"Avignon Nainen" sculpture designed by Markku Salo, with abstract and stylized face in orange and clear glass with overshot and textural surface, mounted in metal stand. *Finland*

Photo by Timo Kauppila courtesy of iittala

"Dogs" designed by Markku Salo in 2000 for Nuutajarvi Pro Arte, colorful bottle-dogs in standing and sitting positions on wire legs. *Finland*

Photo by Timo Kauppila courtesy of iittala

Flygsfors face vases designed by Wiktor Berndt ca. 1960, in deep amber with facial features in relief, signed. *Sweden* Height 8 in; 20.3 cm. $300-400 each

Kosta Boda "Open Minds" series designed by Ulrica Hydman-Vallien in 1987, fantastic cat-like faces painted on colored vases with ears. *Sweden*

Photo courtesy of Kosta Boda

Kosta Boda painted snake designed by Ulrica Hydman-Vallien. *Sweden*

Photo courtesy of Kosta Boda

Kosta Boda "Frutteria" designed by Gunnel Sahlin in 1990, large yellow bowl with blown fruits. *Sweden*

Photo courtesy of Kosta Boda

Kosta Boda Atelier (limited edition) decanter designed by Monica Backstrom in lemon yellow with fruit and green leave stopper, signed and labeled. *Sweden* Height 8-1/2 in; 21.6 cm. $300-400

Detail.

Top Left:
Nuutajarvi Notsjo rooster decanter designed by Kaj Franck and produced from 1955 to 1968, green bottle with rooster stopper in mottled grays. *Finland*
$1000-1500
Photo by Timo Kauppila courtesy of iittala

Bottom Left:
Royal Copenhagen decanter in clear with pink elephant stopper, signed. *Denmark*
Height 9 in; 23 cm.
$150-200

Top Right:
Nuutajarvi Notsjo bottle designed by Kaj Franck ca. 1955, with cube body and hen cork stopper, in grey glass with mottled blue and green spots, signed. *Finland*
Height 6 in; 15.25 cm
$700-800

Bottom Right:
Studioglas Strombergshyttan bird decanters, designed by Anna Ornberg ca. 1988, in lime green with blue spots and round blue bird head stoppers, signed. *Sweden*
Height 13-1/2 in; 34.3 cm.
$200-250 each

Sea Glasbruk "Birdie" series designed by Lena
Engman, whimsical bowls and vases in the form
of birds with applied wings and beaks in orange,
yellow, and cobalt blue. *Sweden*

Photo courtesy of Sea Glasbruk

iittala Blue Magpie designed by Oiva Toikka
in 2000, cobalt blue standing bird with
white head. *Finland*
$300

Photo by Timo Kauppila courtesy of iittala

iittala Common Teals, female and male, designed by Oiva Toikka in 1998, sitting birds in silver and yellow. *Finland*
female $180; male $225

Photo by Timo Kauppila courtesy of iittala

iittala Curlew designed by Oiva Toikka in 1998, seated water bird with black and brown feathery pattern.
$365

Photo by Timo Kauppila courtesy of iittala

Nuutajarvi Notsjo duck with deep teal blue head and black body, designed in 1963, signed.
Finland
Length 5 in; 12.7 cm.
$100-125

Konst Glashyttan red bird figurine. *Sweden*
Length 6 in; 15.25 cm.
$50-75

Riihimaki "Rantakivet" paperweight designed by
Helena Tynell, with molded abstract landscape,
label. *Finland*
$50-75

Yellow mottled miniature bird figures.
Length 2 in; 5 cm.
$15-20 each

FM Ronneby sailing ship by the Marcolin brothers, in clear glass with blues and purples, signed. *Sweden*
Height 9 in; 23 cm.
$125-175

Boda candle holders and little bowls, designed by Erik Hoglund, in opalescent
blue with molded motifs of anchors and dog or maybe a cat. *Sweden*
Diameters 2-3/4 and 3-1/2 in; 7 and 9 cm.
$60-80 each

 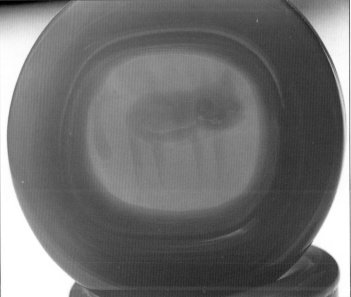

Details.

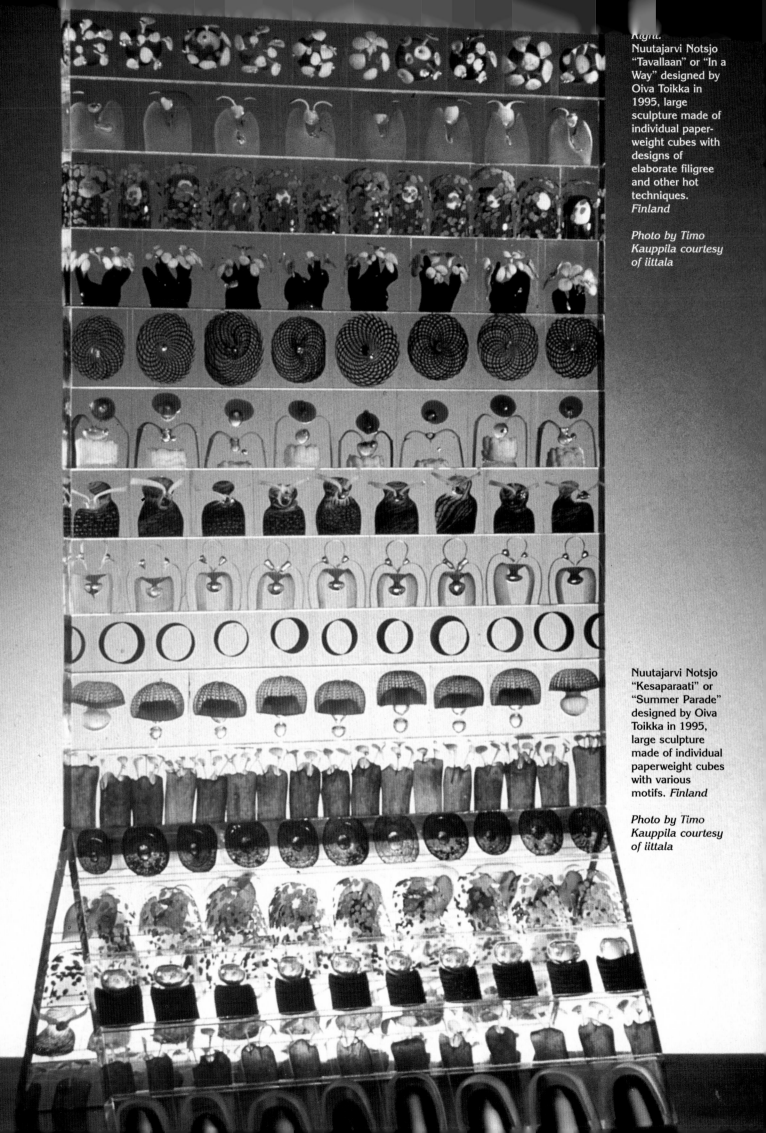

Nuutajarvi Notsjo "Helenan Kylpyamme" or "Helen's Bath" designed by Oiva Toikka in 1987, large sculpture made of individual paperweight cubes enclosing fantastic undersea and other plant and animal forms. This sculpture was shown in the Scandinavian Craft Today exhibition in Japan and the United States in 1987. *Finland*

Photo by Timo Kauppila courtesy of iittala

Detail. Single cube from "Helenan Kylpyamme," signed Nuutajarvi Notsjo 1981 433/1000 Oiva Toikka *Finland* Height 3 in; 7.6 cm. $400-600

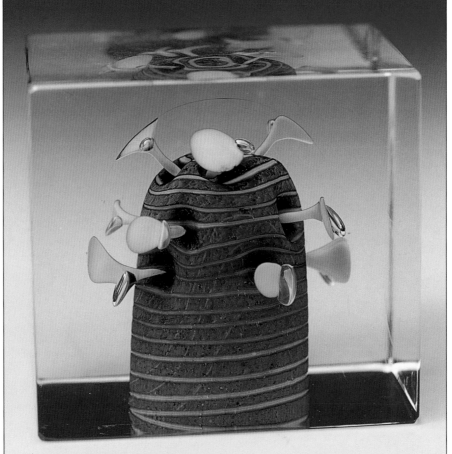

Opposite: Nuutajarvi "Syva Uni" or "The Big Sleep", an installation designed by Annaleena Hakatie in 1998. *Finland*

Photo by Seppo Hilpo courtesy of iittala

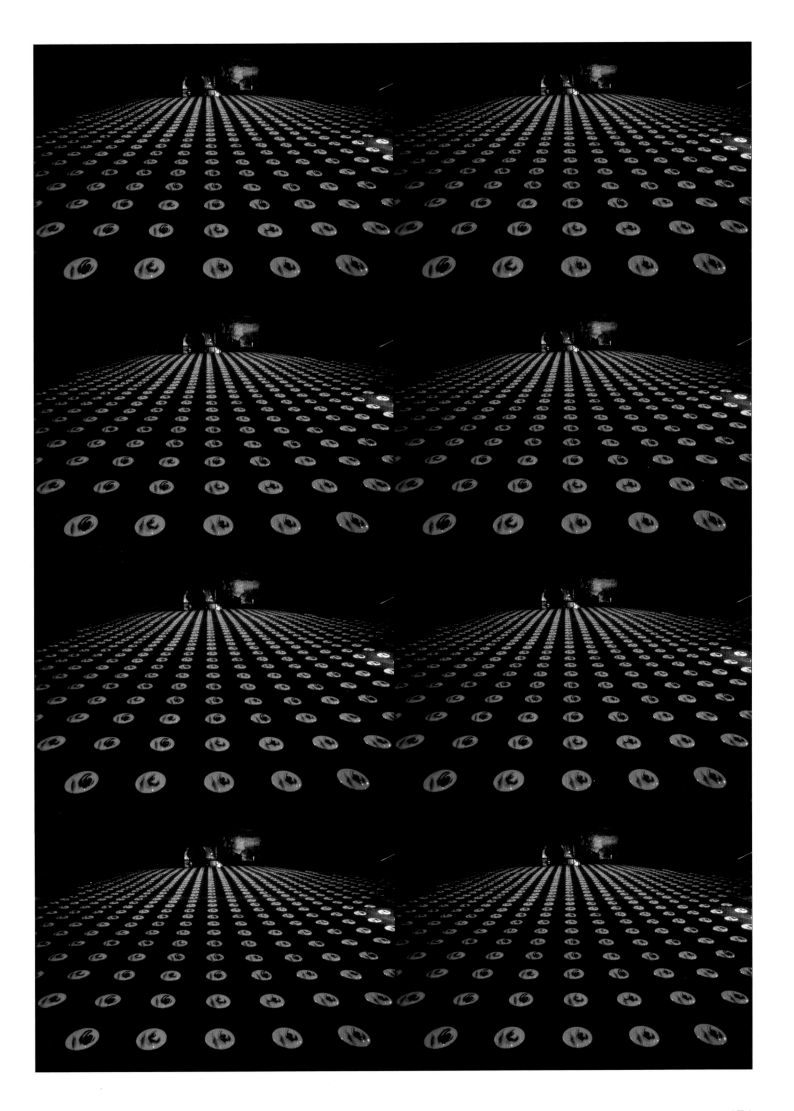

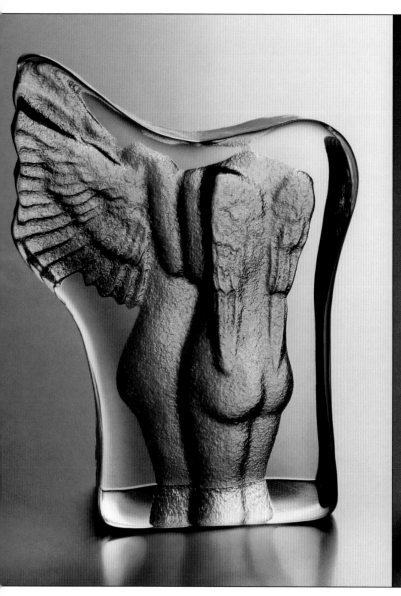

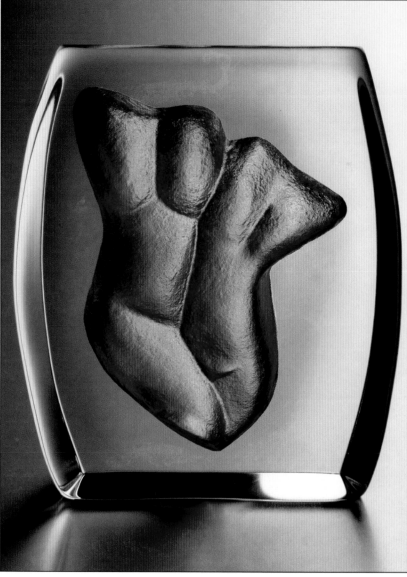

Mats Jonasson Maleras "Arome" sculpture from the "Artemiss" series designed by Erika Hoglund. *Sweden*

The "Artemiss" series consists of 20 sculptures depicting female bodies, and are inspired by the mythological protectress and goddess of wild animals. These sculptures are cast and hand painted. The series is still in production at Mats Jonasson Maleras today.
$150-200

Photo courtesy of Mats Jonasson Maleras

Mats Jonasson Maleras "Plura" sculpture from the "Artemiss" series designed by Erika Hoglund. *Sweden*
$875-1000

Photo courtesy of Mats Jonasson Maleras

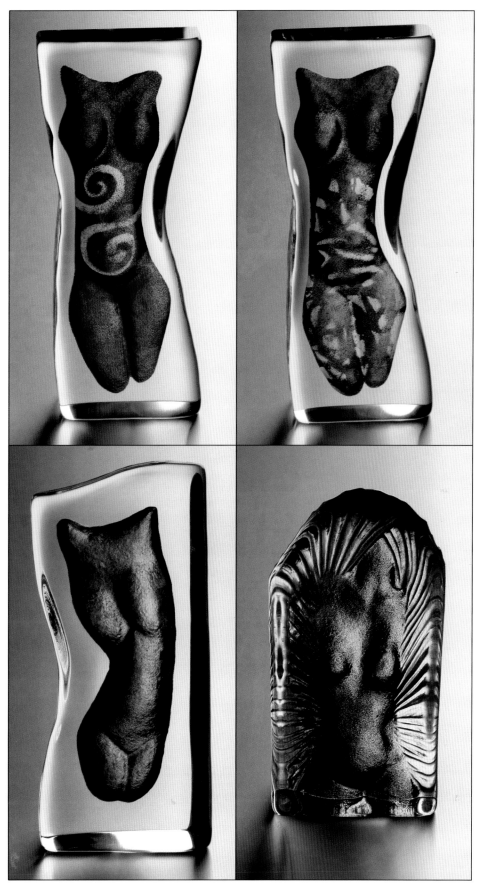

Top Left:
Mats Jonasson Maleras "Uma" sculpture
from the "Artemiss" series designed by Erika
Hoglund. *Sweden*
$450-500
Photo courtesy of Mats Jonasson Maleras

Top Right:
Mats Jonasson Maleras "Jura" sculpture from the
"Artemiss" series designed by Erika Hoglund.
Sweden
$450-500
Photo courtesy of Mats Jonasson Maleras

Bottom Left:
Mats Jonasson Maleras "Maeve" sculpture
from the "Artemiss" series designed by Erika
Hoglund. *Sweden*
$375-425
Photo courtesy of Mats Jonasson Maleras

Bottom Right:
Mats Jonasson Maleras "Diamanda" sculpture
from the "Artemiss" series designed by Erika
Hoglund. *Sweden*
$325-375
Photo courtesy of Mats Jonasson Maleras

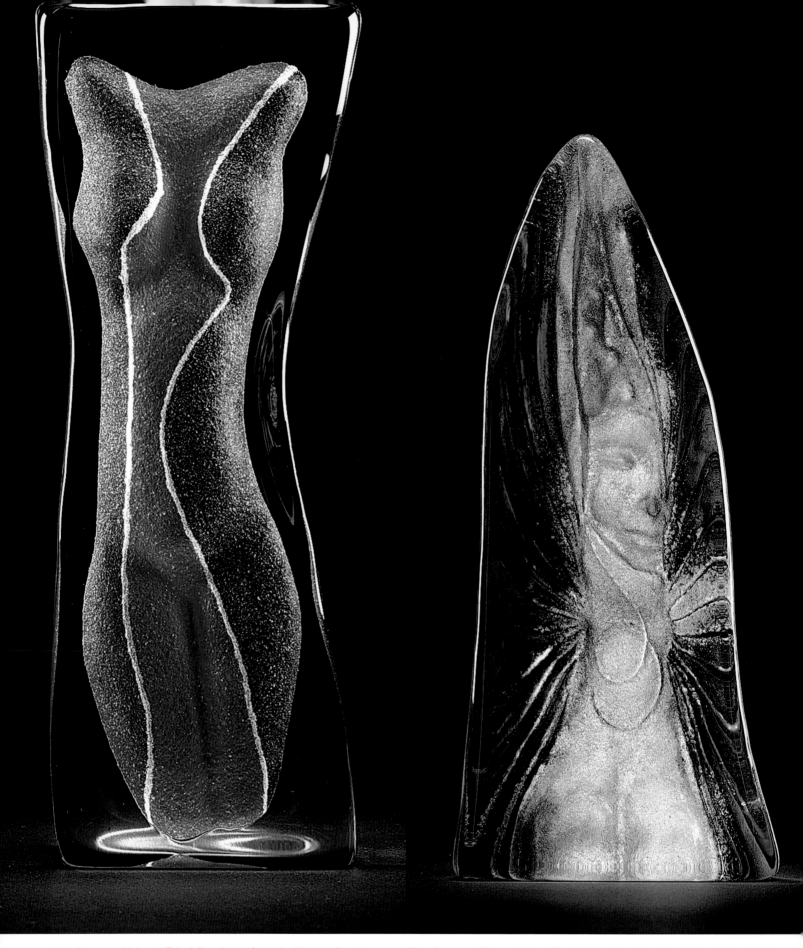

Mats Jonasson Maleras "Fabiola" sculpture from the "Artemiss" series designed by Erika Hoglund. *Sweden*
$475-525

Photo courtesy of Mats Jonasson Maleras

Mats Jonasson Maleras "Miss Affection" sculpture from the "Artemiss" series designed by Erika Hoglund. *Sweden*
$425-475

Photo courtesy of Mats Jonasson Maleras

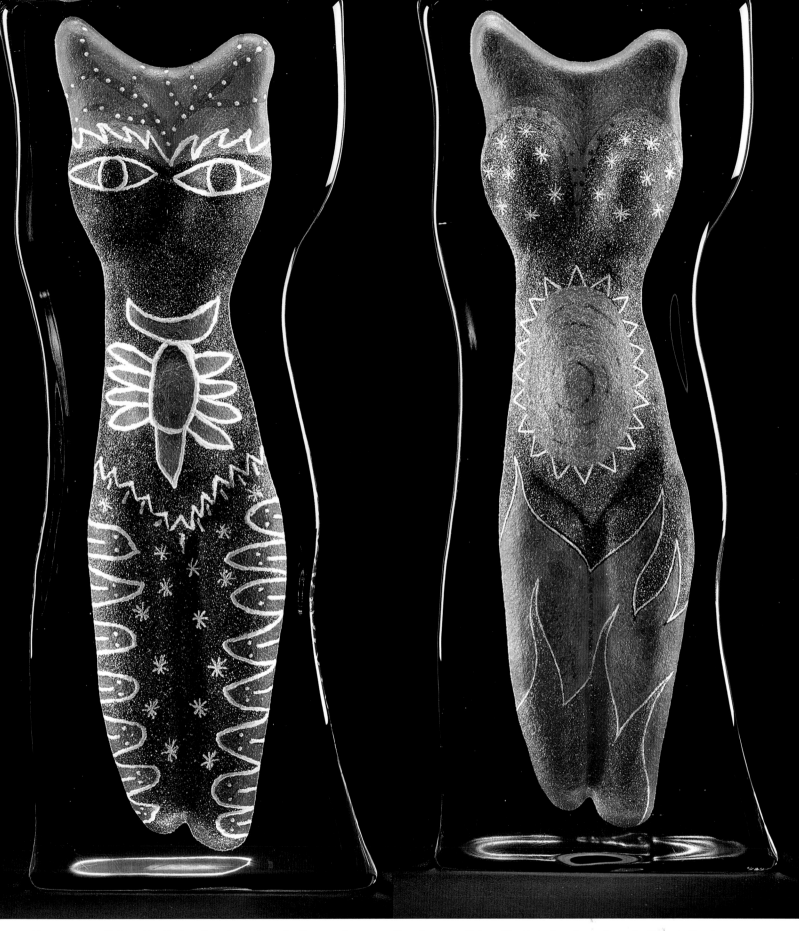

Mats Jonasson Maleras "La Madame" sculpture from the "Artemiss" series designed by Erika Hoglund. This is a limited edition. *Sweden*

Photo courtesy of Mats Jonasson Maleras

Mats Jonasson Maleras "La Merica" sculpture from the "Artemiss" series designed by Erika Hoglund. This is a limited edition. *Sweden*

Photo courtesy of Mats Jonasson Maleras

Chapter 10 • Table

Nuutajarvi Notsjo designs by Kaj Franck, 1950s. *Finland*

Photo courtesy of iittala

Kastrup decanters in red and violet with cork stoppers painted white, designed by Jacob Bang in the early 1960s, Kastrup and Raymor import labels. *Denmark* Heights 13-1/2 and 18-1/2 in; 34.3 and 47 cm. $250-350 each

Gullaskruf opaque pumpkin-orange decanters with contrasting
glass stoppers. *Sweden*
Heights 10-1/2, 14-1/2 and 19 in; 26.7, 37, and 48 cm.
$200-300 each

Boda opaque orange decanters with transparent orange stoppers, designed by Erik
Hoglund ca. 1960s, signed. *Sweden*
Heights 8-3/4 and 10-3/4 in; 22.2 and 27.3 cm.
$250-350 each

Holmegaard "Lava" mottled coffee brown decanter with ground stopper and opening, designed by Per Lutken in 1969, signed.
Denmark
Height 8-1/4 in; 21 cm.
$250-300

Pukeberg "Tropico" decanter designed by Goran Warff in the early 1960s, in double gourd form with teak stopper, with sky blue top blending into grass green bottom, label. *Sweden*
Height 13 in; 33 cm.

Pukeberg "Tropico" decanters designed by Goran Warff in the early 1960s, resembling male and female human figures, in deep sea blue tones, teak stoppers, and two different labels. *Sweden*
Heights without stoppers 10-3/4 and 12 in; 27.3 and 30.5 cm.
With stoppers 11-1/4 and 13 in; 28.6 and 33 cm.
$155-200 each

Holmegaard decanters in sculptural wavy shape, in cobalt blue and emerald green with corks, label. *Denmark*
Heights 6 in; 15.25 cm.
$ 150-200 each

Aseda golden wheat decanter, designed by Bo Borgstrom ca. 1960s, with crystal log stopper, label. *Sweden*
Height 12 in; 30.5 cm.
$100-150

Kosta Boda Artist Collection 'Terrazzo' decanter designed by Ann Wahlstrom in 1994, in lemon yellow double gourd shape with blue droplet stopper with red base, signed. *Sweden*
Height 10-1/4 in; 26 cm.
$300-350

Kastrup decanter likely designed by Jacob Bang ca. 1960s, in cobalt blue with crystal ball stopper, label. *Denmark*
Height 9 in; 23 cm.
$150-175

Holmegaard "Cluck Cluck" bottle decanters, shown in the1950 Holmegaard product catalog, in various sizes and shades of blue and green, one of the most popular and classic designs, with labels. *Denmark*
Heights 9 to 11 in; 23 to 28 cm.
$50-150 each depending on size and color

Riihimaen Lasi "Tippa" decanter set designed by Helena Tynell in 1964, wheel-shaped decanter with double spout and glass in heavy crystal with applied purple disc on each piece, signed. *Finland*
Height 9-1/2 in; 24.1 cm.
$700-900 set

Afors decanter with shot glass stopper and glasses in steel blue, label. Sweden
Height 6-1/2 in; 16.5 cm.
$250-300 set

Gullaskruf decanter with shot glass stopper and matching
shot glasses, in aqua, label. *Sweden*
Height 7 in; 17.8 cm.
$250-300 set

Gullaskruf decanter set in green, designed by Kjell
Blomberg in the late 1950s, shown at the milestone exhibit
"Glass 1959" held at the Corning Museum of Glass, label.
Height 11 in; 28 cm.
$250-350 set

Aseda decanter sets designed by Bo Borgstrom ca. 1960s, in inky blue and golden wheat colors, with clear stoppers
and ornate foot on glasses and decanter, label. *Sweden*
Height 10-1/2 in; 26.7 cm.
$150-200 set

Aseda decanters designed by Bo Borgstrom ca. 1960s, with round stomach bulge like a snake that swallowed an animal, in lime green and golden wheat. *Sweden* Height 11 in; 28 cm. $60-80 each

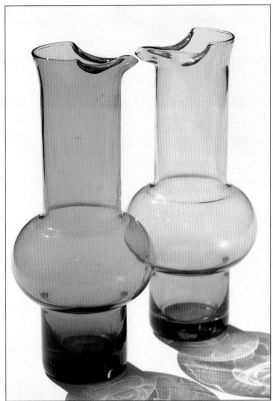

Golden Crown E & R (Aseda) decanter set designed by Bo Borgstrom ca. 1960s, in golden wheat, heavy ornate form with hot decoration and clear foot, label. Golden Crown E & R is an import company. *Sweden* Height 8-1/2 in; 21.6 cm. $ 150-200 set

Aseda decanter sets designed by Bo Borgstrom ca. 1960s, in moss green and inky blue, each with thin glass decanter in a variety of forms, labels. *Sweden*
Heights 8 to 9-3/4 in; 20.3 to 24.75 cm.
$150-200 each set

Humppila smokestack decanter and footed cone-shaped glasses in amber, likely designed in the 1970s, labels. *Finland*
Height 7 in; 17.8 cm.
$150-200 set

Aseda decanter sets designed by Bo Borgstrom ca. 1960s, in amber, each with thin glass decanter in a variety of forms, labels. *Sweden*
Heights 8 to 9-3/4 in; 20.3 to 24.75 cm.
$150-200 each set

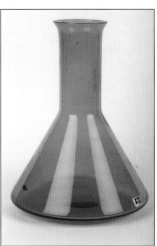

Top:
iittala "Kartio" decanters and glasses in varied sea colors, designed by Kaj Franck in 1958.
Although the "Kartio" series was originally produced at Nuutajarvi Notsjo, it is still in production
today at iittala. *Finland*
$100-150 decanter

Photo by Timo Kauppila courtesy of iittala

Bottom:
iittala "Kartio" decanters and glasses in varied sea colors, designed by Kaj Franck in 1958.

Photo by Gero Mylius courtesy of iittala

Aseda decanter or beaker in
turquoise glass with polished
rim, designed by Bo Borgstrom
ca. 1960s. *Sweden*
Height 8 in; 20.3 cm.
$60-80

Top Left:
Aqua blue handled pitcher and tall cylindrical tumblers, likely Swedish.
Height 9-1/2 in; 24.1 cm.
$125-150 set

Bottom Left:
Royal blue and aqua blue pinched decanters with molded mark "made in Sweden."
Height 8-1/2 in; 21.6 cm.
$40-50 each

Top Right:
Nuutajarvi Notsjo teal pitcher with purple handle, designed by Oiva Toikka, signed. *Finland*
Height 8-1/2 in; 21.6 cm.
$300-350

Bottom Right:
Orrefors cased sapphire blue pitcher in three-part form with sweeping handle, signed and labeled. *Sweden*
Height 16 in; 41cm.
$200-250

Nuutajarvi Notsjo pitchers and glassware, designed by Kaj Franck in the 1950s, in various bright colors. *Finland*

Photo courtesy of iittala

Nuutajarvi Notsjo pitchers, bottles, and other tableware in red, designed by Kaj Franck in 1975. *Finland*
$300-600 each depending on shape and size

Photo courtesy of iittala

iittala "i-lasi" glasses
designed by Timo
Sarpaneva in 1955 and
produced from 1955-
1966. *Finland*

Photo courtesy of iittala

iittala "Kartio" drinkware
series designed by Kaj
Franck in 1958, in colors
of the sea. *Finland*

Photo courtesy of iittala

iittala "Kartio" drinkware series designed by Kaj Franck in 1958, in colors of the sea. *Finland*

Photo by Markku Alatalo courtesy of iittala

iittala "Boy" glassware, designed by Stefan Lindfors
in 1999 in colors of the sea. *Finland*

Photo by Antti Hallakorpi courtesy of iittala

iittala "Verna" stemware, designed by Kerttu Nurminen in 1998, in cool
blues and green. *Finland*

Photo by Markku Alatalo courtesy of iittala

Kumela tumblers in clear blue, label.
Finland
Height 3 in; 7.6 cm.
$10-15 each

Denby canary yellow stems, the same pattern used by Elvis Presley.
$20-25 each

Gullaskruf stemware in cobalt blue.
Sweden
$15-20 each

Denby Milnor tumblers and goblets in wheat color, label. *Sweden*
$15-20 each

Bjorkshult tumblers in opaque black glass, labels. *Sweden*
$20-25 each

Aseda wine glasses designed by Bo Borgstrom ca, 1960s, in amber with green Vaseline foot. *Sweden*
Height 5-1/4 in; 13.3 cm.
$20-25 each

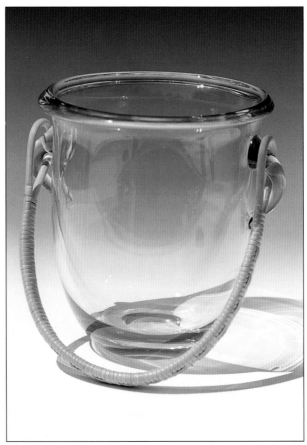

Nuutajarvi Notsjo footed tumbler in wheat
color, label. *Finland*
Height 8-3/4 in; 22.2 cm.
$75-125

Holmegaard bucket, designed by Per Lutken, in icy blue with
wrapped wicker handle, signed. *Denmark*
Height 8-1/2 in; 21.6 cm.
$125-150

Holmegaard handled porringer in moss green with
crystal handle, label. *Denmark*
Length 8-1/2 in; 21.6 cm.
$60-75

Kumela handled dippers in moss green with crystal handles, labels.
Finland
Height
$40-60 each

Gullaskruf compote in aqua blue with simple elongated pedestal and shallow bowl, with label. *Sweden*
Height 9-1/2 in; 24.1 cm.
$75-125

Maleras compote in simple cone and half moon form in aqua blue, with label. *Sweden*
Height 6 in; 15.25 cm.
$60-80

Aseda footed bowl, designed by Bo Borgstrom ca. 1960s, in cobalt blue with green foot, label. *Sweden*
Diameter 7 in; 17.8 cm.
$70-90

Aseda footed bowls in honey and sea blue, with clear foot, label. *Sweden*
Diameters 6-1/4 and 5-1/2 in; 16 and 14 cm.
$30-40 each

Boda plate and covered jar in
light aqua glass and teak lid,
label. *Sweden*
Height
$60-80

Sea Glasbruk opalescent pale
blue compote designed by
Bjorn Ramel, with heavy clear
stem, signed. *Sweden*
Diameter 10-3/4 in; 27.3 cm.
125-150

Boda heavy bubbly blown bottle, pokal, and small
container, designed by Erik Hoglund in the late 1950s,
in amber; signed with H and model numbers. *Sweden*
Heights 6-1/4, 9-1/2, and 3-3/4 in; 16, 24, and 9.5 cm.
$200-250; 150-200; 60-90

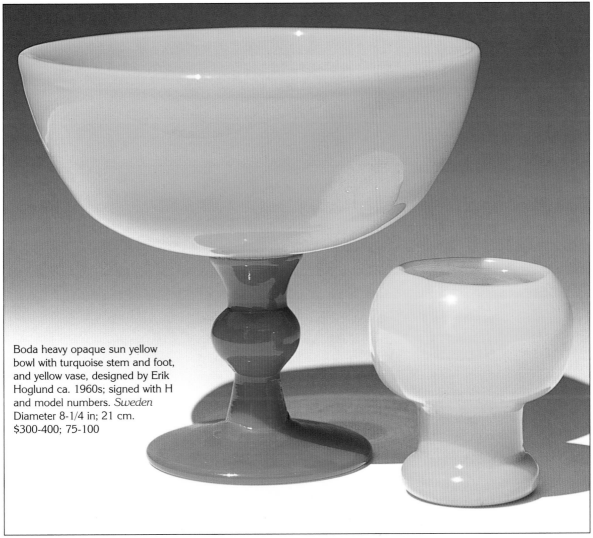

Boda heavy opaque sun yellow
bowl with turquoise stem and foot,
and yellow vase, designed by Erik
Hoglund ca. 1960s; signed with H
and model numbers. *Sweden*
Diameter 8-1/4 in; 21 cm.
$300-400; 75-100

Boda heavy bubbly blown stemware, designed by
Erik Hoglund in the late 1950s, in blood red;
signed with H and model numbers. *Sweden*
Heights 9-1/4 and 6-3/4 in; 23.5 and 17.1 cm.
$250-300; 150-200

Boda heavy bubbly blown stemware,
designed by Erik Hoglund in the late
1950s, in cobalt blue; signed with H
and model numbers. *Sweden*
Heights 6 and 9 in; 15.25 and 23 cm.
$150-200; 250-300

Boda heavy blown stemware in opaque pumpkin orange, designed by Erik
Hoglund ca. 1960s; signed with H and model numbers. *Sweden*
Heights 9 and 7 in; 23 and 18 cm.
$300-350; 200-250

Boda heavy blown bowls in opaque opalescent pumpkin orange, designed by Erik Hoglund ca. 1960s; signed with H and model numbers. *Sweden*
Heights 9-1/4 and 6-3/4 in; 23.5 and 17 cm.
$300-350; 150-200

Orrefors "Colora" bowls designed by Sven Palmqvist around 1954, in opaque sun yellow and Halloween orange, with molded Orrefors signature and label. *Sweden*
Diameter 4-1/2 in; $70-90 each

Orrefors cased bowl with
white exterior and
pistachio green interior,
label. *Sweden*
Diameter 6-1/4 in;
$125-150

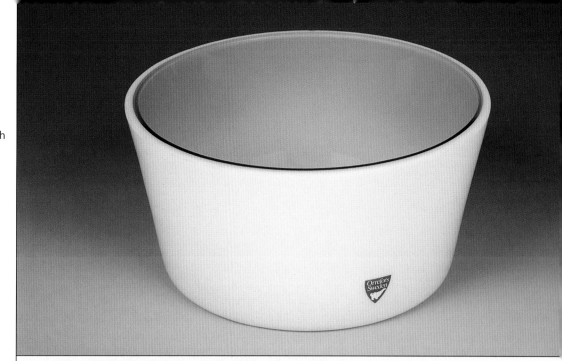

Nuutajarvi Notsjo
"Kastehelmi" tableware
designed by Oiva
Toikka in 1964, in grass
green and sky blue, with
regular pattern of solid
bubbles. *Finland*

*Photo by Gero Mylius
courtesy of iittala*

Nuutajarvi Notsjo blown
bowls, designed by Kaj
Franck in the 1950s in
various colors. *Finland*

Photo courtesy of iittala

Orrefors cased candleholders in turquoise blue and olive green, label. *Sweden*
Heights 2, 4, and 5 in; 5, 10, and 12 cm.
$75-125 each

Pukeberg candleholders in solid green glass,
label. *Sweden*
$20-30 each

Candleholders in painted white metal with round
red discs, marked made in Sweden.
Height 6-1/2 in;
$20-30 each

Opposite Top: iittala "Ballo"
votive candle holders, designed
by Annaleena Hakatie in 1995, in
clear and sea blues. *Finland
Photo by Markku Alatalo,
courtesy of iittala*

Opposite Bottom: iittala "Kivi"
votive candle holders, designed
by Heikki Orvola in 1988. *Finland
Photo courtesy of iittala*

iittala "Kivi" votive candle holders, designed by Heikki Orvola
in 1988. *Finland*

Photo courtesy of iittala

Companies

Afors

Afors was founded in 1876 by four master glassblowers, C. F. Fagerlund, Oscar Fagerlund, Alfred Fagerlund and Carl C. Carlsson, in the Smaland district of Sweden. In 1916, Ernst Johansson, a wholesale merchant, and Oscar Johansson, proprietor of Hjartsjo glassworks purchased the company. In 1917 Ernst Johansson became the sole owner. The glassworks soon passed to Ernst's son, Eric, who changed his last name to Afors. Eric Afors retained control of the company until 1975. In 1964, Afors began a cooperative alliance with 2 other glass factories, Kosta and Boda, and together they were named the Afors group in 1971. In 1972, the Afors group also purchased Johansfors. In 1975, the group was sold to Upsala-Ekeby, the Swedish ceramics concern and in 1976 the Afors group was renamed Kosta Boda AB. In 1982 AB Proventus acquired Kosta Boda's entire stock of shares. In 1990 Kosta Boda merged with Orrefors, becoming Orrefors Kosta Boda. In 1997, Orrefors Kosta Boda became part of The Royal Scandinavia Group, which currently owns a number of companies including Holmegaard, Orrefors, Kosta Boda, Boda Nova, Hoganas Keramik AB (until 2002), Georg Jensen, Royal Copenhagen and Venini.

Early production included mainly household and domestic wares, but in 1910, it expanded to include cut, painted, and etched glass. Bohemian artists such as Karl Zenkert and Karl Diessner helped make Afors renowned in the glass painting technique, which was discontinued in the 1940s. For a short period of time during the 1930s, Astrid Rietz and Edvin Ollers worked for the company. In 1953, designer Ernest Gordon joined the company. In 1963, he was succeeded by Bertil Vallien who experimented with hot-glass ornamentation, sand-blasting techniques and sand-casting. In the 1970s, Afors started its "Artist Collection" to introduce art glass manufactured in small quantities, falling somewhere between unique design and the standard line of glassware. In 1972 his wife, Ulrica Hydman-Vallien, a ceramist, joined Bertil Vallien. She began designing glass for Afors, primarily limited edition studio pieces, but later expanded into designing full lines. She is credited with reviving the practice and tradition of painted glass at Afors, which she currently continues to use at Kosta Boda. Other designers at Afors during the 1980s included Australian Ken Done and Jerker Persson. In 1986, Gunnel Sahlin joined the company as a glass designer, and like the Valliens, she has a studio close to the glassworks. Olle Brozen joined the design team at Kosta Boda in 2000, and he has his studio at Afors.

Because of the long history of mergers and alliances in the Afors group, signatures and markings can sometimes be confusing. Although the literature reports that, since the creation of Kosta Boda AB in 1976, all wares were marketed under the "Kosta Boda" name, in actuality, this is not so. After 1976, some products were still marketed under the "Boda" name only, with signatures and labels to match, and without a reference to "Kosta Boda." Some wares designed as late as 1982-1983, such as the "Rainbow" line by Bertil Vallien, are often found with the "Boda" label and signature. As far as we can discern, sometime between 1984 and 1986, the signatures became uniform, regardless of the factory in which they were produced (Afors, Boda or Kosta) and had both the artist name and the "Kosta Boda" name. Web site: www.kostaboda.com

Alsterfors

Originally an iron foundry, Alsterfors started producing glass in 1885. Around that same time, J.A. Gottwald Fogelberg, the manager at Kosta, purchased it. In 1903, the company became part of the Association of Swedish Crystal Manufacturers and changed hands many times after that. In 1980, it was leased to Orrefors. Production was discontinued in 1980.

Early production included mostly domestic wares and small items, although production expanded to include tableware, restaurant ware and art glass. After 1958, Alsterfors began to produce glass in a variety of colors. Designers associated with the company include Edvin Ollers (1930-1934), Ingrid Atterberg (1958-1964), Fabian Lundkvist (starting in 1960) and P. O. Strom (1968-1972). While most of Alsterfors wares are rarely signed and only labeled, many designs by P. O. Strom from the late 1960s and early 1970s include his signature and year of production.

Aseda

Aseda glass of Sweden produced a wide variety of unusual shapes, often with a heavy paperweight type base. Sometimes the base is a contrasting color from the body of the vase. Colors ranged from subdued earthy tones to vibrant reds, oranges, and yellows, which were also made in a semi-opaque, opalescent type glass. The primary designer of these playful sixties forms was ceramist and glass designer, Bo Borgstrom. Before joining Aseda in 1955, Borgstrom studied in Stockholm as well as other European and American cities. A silver foil on paper label has black lettering that is often mistaken as "Seda." In 1974, Aseda became part of the Royal Krona Group (Krona-Bruken AB), which consisted of other four companies: Bjorkshult, Gullaskruf, Maleras, and Skruf. The Royal Krona group went bankrupt in 1977.

Bergdala

Bergdala was founded in 1889, in Sweden's Smaland region. Bergdala is currently associated with Skruf and Alghult, and together create the Svenska Glasbruk Group. Bergdala is best known for its designs in clear glass with applied cobalt blue glass edges. Current designers for the company include, Thommy Bremberg, Sven Lidberg, Christoffer Ramsey, Lena Linderholm, Eva-Lena Martinsson, and Mats Theselius.

Bjorkshult

Originally called Bjorkklunda, the glassworks was founded in 1892 by three master glassblowers- Carl L. Petersson, F. Oscar Johansson and Oscar Carlstrom- and a glasscutter, E. Robert Nyrena. By 1919, the company had changed hands four times, and was finally re-named Bjorkshult. In 1925, confounded by many economic problems, two members of the Scheutz family invested capital in the company, in order to make improvements. In 1934, the company was sold to 3 glassblowers who modernized the plant by adding a new blowing room. By 1974 the company became part of the Krona-Bruken AB and ceased production in 1978.

Early production consisted of domestic tableware and ornamental glass, but soon began to produce cut crystal. By 1930, production of "stable glass" began. This was a high and toughened grade of glass used for airport lights, but also used in tableware production. During the 1940s, Ragnar Johansson, a glassblower, began designing animals in glass. In the 1950s, the primary designers were Hans-Christian Wagner (1957-1976), Margareta Schlyter-Stiernstedt (1953-1968) and Carl-Einar Borgstrom (1970s). During 1973 and until it's closing, Bjorkshult produced glassware common to the Krona-Bruken AB (Royal Krona).

Boda

R. Wiktor Scheutz and Erik Widlund, two glass blowers from Kosta, founded Boda in 1864 in the Smaland region of Sweden. In 1947, Boda was acquired by Eric Afors, owner of the Afors glass factory, but was independently run and managed by Erik Rosen. In 1964, Boda began a cooperative alliance with Kosta and Afors, and in 1971, all three formally merged into the Afors group. The Afors family sold the company to Upsala-Ekeby in 1975, and a year later the company group was reformed into Kosta Boda AB. In 1990 Kosta Boda merged with Orrefors to create Orrefors Kosta Boda. In 1997, Orrefors Kosta Boda became part of The Royal Scandinavia Group.

Boda's early production was blown and pressed glassware and bottles. Around 1920, crystal was brought into production. Gabriel Burmeister designed art glass for a short period during the 1920s. Fritz Kallenberg designed mass-produced domestic glassware and some individual objects from 1925 to 1968. Boda produced canning jars during World War II but by the end of the 1940s, the standard production line went back into operation. In an effort to bring art glass and sophisticated objects into Boda's production, Erik Hoglund was hired by Erik Rosen as a designer in 1953. Hoglund's distinctive engraved crystal and colored seedy glass with imaginative applications brought a new trend to Swedish glass. Hoglund remained at Boda until 1973. Other artists who were associated with Boda were, Lena Larsson (1960s), Monica Backstrom (1965-present), Signe Persson-Melin (1967-1973), Rolf Sinnemark (1971-1985), and Kjell Engman (1978-present). Web site: www.kostaboda.com

Dansk

Dansk was the creation of New York entrepreneur/engineer Ted Nierenberg in collaboration with designer Jens Quistgaard. In 1950, Mr. Nierenberg and his wife Martha traveled to Denmark, and at Copenhagen's Kundstanvaark Museum, saw a hand-forged fork, spoon, and knife with teakwood handles that had won a design competition for 35-year-old Jens Quistgaard. Quistgaard

believed that his designs were too difficult to manufacture, and no one wanted to tackle them. But Nierenberg's search led him to manufacturing sources he knew could execute such pieces. He convinced Quistgaard that they had to try. The pattern was Fjord, now considered a classic of modern Scandinavian flatware design. Dansk has specialized in the design of "table top" items, always with the idea that every object needed for the top of the table can be beautiful as well as useful.

Dansk continues to produce numerous items in glass, wood, silver, and pottery. Designs created by Jens Quistgaard can be identified by his initials "JHQ", or the letters "IHQ", on the labels or marks. Gunnar Cyren also designed for Dansk. His pieces can be identified his initials "GC" on labels or marks.

Ekenas

Founded in Sweden in 1917 by former Orrefors workers, Ekenas was purchased by Sven Westberg in 1922. For forty years, until he died in 1962, Westberg hired talented designers, including the sculptor John-Orwar Lake, who served as chief designer and art director from 1953 to 1976. Danish designer Michael Bang worked briefly for Ekenas in the 1960s. The factory closed in 1976.

Elme

Elme glassworks was founded in 1917 after the Fare glassworks in Sibbhult transferred production to a newly built facility in Almhult, Sweden. The factory was owned and managed by Gustaf Dahlen, a Nobel laureate credited with the creating of gas lit lighthouses, and first production consisted of signal glass and lighthouse lenses manufacturing. After the First World War, due to imports, the company manufactured lighting fixtures. During the 1920s, after bankruptcy and reorganization, the company began to produce blown and pressed domestic glassware.

Edvin Ollers worked at the company from 1926 to 1930 designing quality pressed glass as well as highly engraved and cut art glass. Many of the examples designed in pressed glass by Ollers at that time include his last name and the company name pressed on the bottom of the design. Catalogs show that his design code for the cut and engraved art glass was "O". During the 1930s, Emil Weidlich, a glass engraver who worked at Orrefors from 1922 to 1929, also designed at Elme. His designs were in highly engraved crystal glass and are usually signed "E. Weidlich" or simply "EW" or "W" with a production number. They are often not signed with the engraved "Elme", therefore they can be difficult to identify as an Elme design.

After the recession of the 1930s, the factory was reorganized and sold to Leonard Borgarp in 1938. In 1940, the company changed hands again, but was reacquired by the Borgarp family in 1962. Designers during the 1960s included Carl Olov Borgarp and his wife, Kjeld Jordan, John Hall, Hjordis Olsson (beginning in 1967), and Charlotte Rude. After poor profits, the company closed in 1970.

Flygsfors

The factory was founded in 1888 in the Smaland region of Sweden, by Ernst Wiktor Lundqvist and August Zeitz, mainly to produce window glass. After changing hands several times, handmade window glass production was discontinued in 1920. In 1930, the company was renamed Flygsfors Glasbruk AB and began producing tableware, preserve jars and lighting fixtures. Main production in the 1940s consisted of glass prisms, and domestic and ornamental wares. In 1959, Flygsfors acquired the Gadderas Glassworks and the Maleras Glassworks in 1965. Together they became known as the Flygsfors group. Gadderas soon closed and Maleras became part of the Krona-Bruken AB in 1974. Flygsfors was then acquired by Orrefors and production ceased in 1979.

Paul Kedelv joined Flygsfors in 1949, mainly to design light fixtures, but he is best known today for his sculptural art glass, which included the "Coquille" series. After he left the company in 1956, Marie Bergqvist had a brief tenure. Wiktor Berndt designed lighting fixtures and art glass from 1955 until the takeover by Orrefors. Other designers associated with the company were Hans-Agne Jakobsson (from 1957), Ulla Nordenfeldt (around 1960), Sigvard Bernadotte, and the Finnish glass designer Helena Tynell (in 1968).

Most Flygsfors pieces were signed with company name, designer and year of production, or the company name only. However, some were only signed on the bottom with a small mark, which resembles "Sa" and can be difficult to find. Regardless, most Flygsfors pieces are not difficult to identify by their style, especially if they are part of the "Coquille" range.

FM Konstglas

The company was founded in 1961 in Ronneby, Sweden by two Italian brothers, Josef (Giuseppe) and Benito Marcolin. After training as glass blowers in Murano, the Marcolin brothers ventured to the Smaland region of Sweden in the early 1950s. They worked as glass blowers for a period of time, but then decided to start their own venture, and created FM Konstglas, a company which specialized in hand blown figural pieces which, although Swedish, had a decisively Italian touch to them. In order to increase production at the factory, they were later joined by another brother, Giovanni Luigi, and a sister, Annamaria, who was married to another master glass blower, Aure Toso. The FM initials on the name of the company stand for "Fare Marcolin" or "Made by Marcolin." Their pieces are technically precise, and use many of the techniques that the Marcolin brothers mastered at Murano. They were also wisely marketed worldwide. Forty years after the creation of the company, Josef Marcolin retired and moved back to Italy.

Some of the early FM Konstglas pieces from the 1960s were unsigned and only labeled. However, most of their wares were signed in different ways through the years.

Gullaskruf

Originally a bottle-making company in Sweden's Smaland district from 1893-1921, it reopened in 1927. The new owner, William Stenberg, hired artist Hugo Gehlin in 1930, who became one of Sweden's first designers to work with organic design. He is credited with designing pressed and blown household wares, as well as enameled and free-blown art glass, which gave Gullaskruf a recognizable identity. Arthur Percy joined Gullaskruf in 1951, and stayed until 1965. Kjell Blomberg began designing geometric forms in 1955, and he remained until 1977. Catharina Aselius-Lidbeck also worked at the company from 1968 to 1970. In 1974, the factory became part of Royal Krona Group (Krona-Bruken AB) and in 1977 was leased to Orrefors after Royal Krona Group went bankrupt. Gullaskruf shut down in 1983, reopened in 1990 under new management, and closed again in 1995.

Most of Gullaskruf wares were labeled and unsigned, however, a few signed examples can be found, particularly in wares produced in the 1960s and 1970s, including some designed by Arthur Percy and Kjell Blomberg.

Hadeland

Hadeland Glassworks is both the oldest existing industrial company in Norway and the longest existing glassworks. It was founded in 1762 at Mo in Jevnaker, a site owned the Danish-Norwegian state, and production started in 1765. Its early production was comprised mainly of bottles, glass for the pharmaceutical industry, and household glass. Hadeland became part of a shareholding company in 1898 called A/S Christiania Glasmagasin with two other glass companies, mainly making lighting and window glass.

Sverre Pettersen was appointed the first full-time art designer in 1928 and introduced a modern style to the tableware and art glass. Stale Kyllingstad joined Hadeland in 1937 and introduced sandblasted design techniques. After working as an apprentice for many years, Willy Johansson started as a designer for Hadeland in 1946, later became head designer, and remained there until 1988.

Hadeland has a long list of illustrious designers which include Hermann Bongard (1947-1955), Gerd Slang (1948-1952 and 1963-1972), Arne Jon Jutrem (1950-1962 and 1985-present), Severin Broby (since 1956), Benny Motzfeldt (1955-1967), Gro Bergslien (married name, Sommerfeldt, employed since 1964), and Edla Freij (1970s). Designers during the 1990s include Inger Magnus, Kjell Johannessen, Gro Eriksson Stoll, Kari Ulleberg, Suzanne Schurch and Marketa Burianova. The current chief designer and art director at the company is Maud Gjerulsen Bugge, accompanied by Lena Hansson and Cecilie Moe Sindum, who are full time designers.

In 1982, share turnover was released and Christiania Glasmagasin turned public. Within a few years, the entire company was acquired by Atle Brynestad and divided into a number of smaller companies. Today, Hadeland Glassworks is a separate and independent company, owned by GC Holdings, which also owns Lindshammar Glassworks in Sweden, Steninge Slott, as well as the retailer, Duka.

Hadeland wares are mostly signed and include the designer signature or initials, production numbers and sometimes year of production.

Holmegaard and Kastrup

Countess Henriette Danneskiold-Samsoe founded the Holmegaard glass factory in 1825 near the village of Fensmark, in order to take advantage of the Holmegaard Moors and use peat as a fuel source. For the first ten years, the factory produced bottles for beer and schnapps. In 1835, Holmegaard brought glass blowers from Bohemia and Germany, in order to expand production and to include more domestic items, which they achieved during the latter part of the 19th century.

Holmegaard founded the Kastrup glass factory in 1847, in order to produce bottles for the Copenhagen market, which was only a few kilometers from the factory. In 1873, Kastrup was sold and the new owners started producing several types of tableware and other household items. Around that time, the first pressed glass was made in Denmark at the factory. By the turn of the century, Kastrup was manufacturing popular glassware with etched decorations. In 1907, Kastrup bought the Fyens factory (established in 1874) in the town of Odense, in order to specialize in production of opaline glass, which was used mainly for lampshades.

Until 1965, Holmegaard and Kastrup operated as independent and competing glass factories, but in that year the factories merged to create a single company, Kastrup and Holmegaard. By 1968 the Kastrup glass factory had ceased production of hand blown glass, which was made now only at Holmegaard factory and the Odense factory.

Architect Jacob Bang came to Holmegaard as staff designer in 1927 and brought much attention to the company by designing large collections of art glass. Bang left Holmegaard in 1941 to pursue other interests, but returned in 1957, now as a designer for Kastrup, where he remained until his death in 1965. Per Lutken was hired in 1942, and stayed at Holmegaard as designer and artistic director until his death in 1998. Other designers employed by Kastrup and Holmegaard from the late 1950s to mid-1970s were Christer Holmgren (Holmegaard, 1957-1972), who was joined by his wife Christel Holmgren in later years, Arne Jon Jutrem (Holmegaard, freelance), Grethe Meyer (Kastrup), Ibi Trier Morch (Kastrup), and Bent Severin(Kastrup). In 1968, Michael Bang, the son of Jacob Bang, was hired as a designer for Holmegaard and in the beginning mainly worked at Odense, where he created the "Pallet" series.

During the 1970s, many freelance designers were associated with Holmegaard, including Kylle Svanlund, Britta Strombeck, Sidse Werner, the American designer Joel Philip Myers and the English artist, Annette Meech. In 1979, the Kastrup factory closed. It was around this time that Kastrup and Holmegaard was renamed simply Holmegaard. In 1985, Holmegaard joined the Royal Copenhagen group. The Odense Factory was closed in 1990. In 1997, the Royal Copenhagen group became part of Royal Scandinavia. Holmegaard is still producing glass today and current production includes designs by Per Lutken, Verner Panton, Piet Hein, Michael Bang, Allan Scharff, Anja Kjaer, Mads Odgard, Malene Lutken, Peter Svarrer, Sidse Werner and Torben Jorgensen.

Most of the glass produced at the Kastrup factory was only labeled and unmarked. The wares produced at Holmegaard were mostly signed, many times indicating the designer and year of production.

Humppila

Three brothers, Jonni, Martti and Olavi Helander, who were trained as glassblowers and previously worked at Nuutajarvi, founded Humppila Glassworks in 1952. Initial production consisted of both utilitarian glass and art glass, and during the 1950s the three brothers were also the designers for the company. During the 1950s, designer Sirkku Lehtonen joined them.

In 1970, due to financial problems, the glassworks had to be sold and was purchased by Rolf Alander, who rebuilt the factory and radically changed the direction of production. Under his guidance in the 1970s, the company began producing tableware and art glass that was mostly cast. Designers hired during the 1970s include Henrik Koivula (1969-1986), Pertti Santalahti (1971-1981), Vesa Antikainen (1971-), Tauno Wirkkala (1972-), Kaija Aarikka (1972-1986), Kai Blomqvist (1976-1988) and Hillevi Lalla (1977-). In 1979, Humppila acquired Kumela Glassworks. Taru Syrjanen began working for the company as a designer in 1981. In 1986, Nuutajarvi

acquired Humppila, but production under the Humppila name continued until the late 1980s.

Although glass production has now ceased at the company, Humppila Glassworks can still be visited today. Now owned by iittala, the factory houses shops selling a number of Finnish products and glass is blown on an exhibition basis. Other designers associated with Humppila are Borje Rajalin and Olavi Ruottinen. Many of the pieces produced by Humppila were signed, including some of the early pieces from the 1950s. Web site: www.iittala.com

iittala

In 1881, a Swedish master glass blower, Petter Magnus Abrahamsson, established the iittala Glassworks in Finland. After a difficult start, the factory established its status as a manufacturer of quality products, until the long period of growth was interrupted by the First World War. The first glassblowers came to iittala from Sweden. In the beginning, the majority of its production consisted of simple household glass, with little cut or engraved glass. In 1917, due to the great difficulties of the First World War, the shareholders were compelled to sell the company to Ahlstrom Oy, a group which also owned the glass factory Karhula.

During the 1920s, although Ahlstrom made numerous improvements at iittala, Karhula still played a more important role. During the 1930s, Karhula concentrated on production of bottles and pressed glass while iittala concentrated on blown glass. At that time, the companies arranged glass design competitions to attempt to raise the profile of both utility and art glass. Aino Aalto won second prize at the competition in 1932 and Alvar Aalto took first prize in 1936. The "Aalto" vase, though a Karhula-owned design, was transferred to iittala for manufacture.

Another competition was held in 1946 to discover new engraved glass designs. The outcome of this competition brought Tapio Wirkkala and Kaj Franck to iittala, where both were appointed chief designers. After Franck moved to Nuutajarvi in 1950, Timo Sarpaneva arrived to take his place. In 1956, iittala launched its first modern utility glass collection, designed by Timo Sarpaneva. The "i-collection" or "i-series" arose from a critical demand for modern, functional and beautiful, everyday items. The "i-collection" also carried the "i" label for the first time, which was to become iittala's trademark.

In the 1950s and 1960s, Wirkkala and Sarpaneva won prizes at several competitions, including the Milan Triennales. Through their innovative work, Finnish glass gained an international reputation. iittala's factory underwent major renovation in the 1960s, and utility glassware began to be marketed under the "i" trademark. Production methods were created, including the use of burned wooden molds and engraved graphite molds. A breakthrough came in 1964, with Sarpaneva's popular "Finlandia" collection.

In 1971, iittala opened a glass museum and built a factory for producing lamps and lighting. Valto Kokko, who since 1963 had designed lamp glass, began also to create utility glass. At the end of the 1980s the ownership of the iittala ownership was changed. In 1987, A. Ahlstrom Oy and Wartsila, two large Finnish industrial groups, merged their glass industries into iittala-Nuutajarvi, in order to fight the heavy competition of the ever-growing glass imports.

In 1990, the Hackman Group bought iittala-Nuutajarvi, and the new company continued by the name of "Hackman iittala". By 1994, Hackman combined its various tableware factories (glass, porcelain and stainless steel) into one unit called Hackman Designor Oy Ab. In 2002, the company's name was changed to iittala Oy Ab. Today, iittala Oy Ab has six brands which include Arabia, Hackman, iittala, Rorstrand-Gustavsberg, Hoyang-Polaris (Norway) and the recently acquired Boda Nova-Hoganas Keramik Ab (Sweden) in 2002. Web site: www.iittala.com

iittala's Staff and Freelance designers:

Note that the current designers working at iittala, together with the designers working at Nuutajarvi, comprise iittala's design team, and all wares are marketed under that name.

Aino Aalto	1930s
Alvar Aalto	1930s
Goran Hongell	1932-1957
Erkki Vesanto	1936-1980
Greta-Lisa Jaderholm-Snellman	1945-1962
Gunnel Nyman	1946-1947
Tapio Wirkkala	1946-1985
Kaj Franck	1946-1950
Liisa Johansson-Pape	1948-1960s
Timo Sarpaneva	1950-
Valto Kokko	1963-1993
Jorma Vennola	1975-1986
Mikko Karpannen	1983-1988
Tiina Nordstrom	1988-1997
Kai Blomqvist	1988-
Erkkitapio Siiroinen	1992-1996
Kati Tuomen-Niittyla	1993-
Elina Joensuu	1995
Konstantin Grcic	1998
Stefan Lindfors	1998-
Harri Koskinen	1998-
Marc Newson	1998-
Carina Seth-Anderson	1998-
Antonio Citterio	1998-
Bjorn Dahlstrom	1998-
Alfredo Haberli	1999-
Toan Nguyen	2004-

Other designers associated with iittala are Helja Liukko-Sundstrom, Brita Flanders, Marcus Eerola, and Nathalie Lahdenmaki.

Johansfors

The factory was founded in 1891 in Sweden. One of the founders was F. O. Israelsson, a church warden. From 1904 to 1911, the factory was leased to AB De Svenska Kristallglas-bruken (Association of Crystal Manufacturers), after which it was run by Israelsson. From 1950 to 1972, Sixten Wennerstrand rebuilt and modernized the company. In 1972, Johansfors was sold to the Afors Group (later known as Kosta Boda AB). In 1990, Kosta Boda merged with Orrefors. In 1992 Johansfors was taken over by a group of former employees. The company is still in production and currently owned by the Norwegian glass firm, Magnor.

During the early years of production, Johansfors mainly made pressed glassware and hand painted decorative glass, which later became one of its specialties. During the 1920s, cut glass also became a specialty and several cutters from Kosta and Bohemia

came to the company. In the mid-1920s, four engravers were hired, one of whom, Folke Walwing, later became art director at Maleras. Johansfors cut and engraved wares were very successful internationally. Several commendations were given for its products at the World Exhibition in Barcelona in 1929.

In the 1930s, new products were designed by artist Gunnar Hakansson and Johansfors concentrated and thrived on producing designs by their artists. From 1938 to 1947, many of the designs were made by Gustaff Hallberg, the chief gaffer. In 1952, artist and designer Bengt Orup, started working for the company and was employed until 1973. Orup was rather prolific and designed wares from simple tableware to art glass. Other artists employed at the company were Margareta and Rik Hennix (65-67) and Ingegerd Raman (68-71).

The majority of Johansfors wares were signed, however, some examples can be found without a signature or only labeled.

Karhula

Karhula Glassworks was founded in 1889 by Captain William Ruth. They produced bottles and household glass with designs copied from Nuutajarvi, Reijmyre, and Swedish and German designs. Molded and blown glass production was overseen by a certified master blower, M.A. Kolehmainen, who worked at Karhula from 1899 to 1910. A. Ahlstrom Oy bought Karhula in 1915 and then bought iittala in 1917. Eric O.W. Ehrstrom was a designer and artistic director starting in 1925, and his designs favored lighter, engraved glass. At the Antwerp world exhibition in 1930, Karhula won awards for its designs. Seeking modern design, Karhula-iittala organized design competitions during the 1930s. Successful designers during these competitions included Aino Aalto, Goran Hongell, Arttu Brummer, Antti Salmenlinna, Elmar Granlund, Yrjo Rosola, Aarre Putro, and Lisa Johansson-Pape.

At the Milan Triennale in 1933, Karhula entered all but the pressed glass designs, and the factory won the highest award. After the competition, Goran Hongell was appointed resident artistic designer and held that post until he retired in 1957. One of Hongell's most notable designs, the "Aarne" glass series won a gold medal at the Milan Triennale in 1954. In 1937, another design competition was organized and designers who participated included Gunnel Nyman, Gunilla Jung, Richard Jungell, Yrjo Rosola, Aino and Alvar Aalto, Goran Hongell, Gunnar Forstrom, Erik Bryggman, and Aulis Blomstedt. Alvar Aalto's "Eskimo Woman's Leather Breeches" was the winner and later acquired the name the "Savoy" vase, because of the association of the piece with Helsinki's Savoy restaurant.

Karhula began producing glass containers in 1945 and utilizing bottle-making machines in 1948. Molded glass production and art glass was moved to iittala in 1954, leaving Karhula with fully automated glass container production. Karhula produced glass tiles from the 1930s until 1968. A. Ahlstrom Oy bought Riihimaki glass in 1985 and combined the companies. Riihimaki glass closed in 1990 and in 1995, Karhula was purchased by an American company, Owens-Illinois.

Karhula Glassworks' Staff and Freelance Designers:

Eric O.W. Ehrstrom (Artistic Advisor)	1925
Richard Jungell (Master Cutter)	1920s-1930s

Goran Hongell	1932-1957
Aino Marsio-Aalto	1930s
Alvar Aalto	1930s
Gunnel Nyman	1935-1937
Arttu Brummer	1930s
Gunilla Jung	1930s
Yrjo Rosola	1930s
Frans Rantanen	1930s
Baron Emil Cedercreutz	1930s
Tapio Wirkkala	1960s

Kosta and Kosta Boda

In 1742, two generals in Sweden's army, Anders Koskull and Bogislaus Stael Von Holstein, founded a glass company which they named with letters borrowed from their names "Ko" and "Sta." In 1746, Johan Wickenberg acquired Kosta and it stayed in the family until 1893. The Wickenbergs were excellent managers who expanded sales by opening offices in Stockholm and as far away as Russia.

Early production at Kosta was mainly window glass, including the window glass for the royal palace in Stockholm. Kosta also made chandeliers, bottles for beer and schnapps, and household wares. In 1752, engraved glass began production, in 1828 cut glass was introduced, and in 1889 a glass pressing machine was installed. One of Kosta's specialties in the 1880s was stemware. Much of Kosta's production was exported and it was Sweden's second largest glass producer. Production was modernized to include cut glass, and, in 1833, the first printed price list was published by manager Uno Angerstein. Axel Hummel, a former forestry engineer, became manager in 1887. Hummel put company finances in order, modernized production and helped bring the railway to Kosta in 1890. Kosta hired artist Gunnar Wennerberg to design a series of cut and overlay designs for the Paris Exposition of 1900. Another celebrated artist, Alf Wallander, worked at Kosta during the 1900s.

Kosta realized much acclaim from the work of Wennerberg and Wallander and recognized the value of collaboration between artists. Artists who worked for Kosta during the 1920s and 1930s included Karl Hulstrom, Sten Branzell, Ewald Dahlskog, Sven Erixson, Erik Skawonius, Tyra Lundgren, and Edvin Ollers. Elis Bergh was art director at Kosta from 1929 to 1950. He began designing light fixtures, but soon started producing bowls, vases, and stemware.

In 1950, Vicke Lindstrand took over for Bergh. Lindstrand had a gift for bold experimentation and for the creation of art glass techniques. In addition to art glass with new shapes and colors, he is noted for his stemware and even designed glass for public spaces. In the 1960s, Mona Morales-Schildt designed the elegant "Ventana" pieces using a cut overlay technique and several new and young artists found a place at Kosta. These included Sigurd Persson, Lisa Bauer, Rolf Sinnemark, and Ann and Goran Warff. Since the artists who came in the 1960s did such notable and impressive work, Kosta followed suit in the 1970s, hiring Paul Hoff, Bengt Edenfalk, Anna Ehrner, and Klas-Goran Tinback. Since the 1980s, Kosta has produced many series of bowls, vases, and tableware alongside art glass that has brought acclaim both in Sweden and abroad.

In 1964 Kosta began a cooperative alliance with two other glass factories, Afors and Boda, and together they were named the Afors group in 1971. In 1972, the Afors group also purchased Johansfors. In 1975, the group was sold to Upsala-Ekeby, the Swedish ceramics concern, and in 1976 the Afors group was renamed Kosta Boda AB. In 1982 the Kosta Boda's entire stock of shares was acquired by AB Proventus. In 1990 Kosta Boda merged with Orrefors, becoming Orrefors Kosta Boda. In 1997, Orrefors Kosta Boda became part of The Royal Scandinavia Group.

During the early 1950s and 1960s, most pieces were marked "Kosta," with a designer code, followed by a secondary code, which indicated the type of glass, and a four-digit production number. These codes were used to resemble those used by Orrefors. The known designer codes during this time are included in the list of designers. The codes for designs by Vicke Lindstrand during the 1950s and 1960s were as follows:

LH Hand-shaped glass
LU "Unica" design
LC Hand-shaped glass in the "Colora" technique
LF Hand-shaped bird sculptures
LG Engraved glass
LS Cut glass

During the early 1970s, the signatures and markings at Kosta changed to include the designers' signatures, as well as a 5 digit production number. This seems to coincide with the creation of the Afors group. The change to 5 digits is significant because, around 1974, the year of design could be identified with the second and third digit of the production number. The first digit indicates the type of ware, for example, vase codes would always start with a 4, bowl codes would start with a 5, candleholders with a 6, plates with a 7, and decanters with an 8. The identification of year of design holds true for most wares except for stemware, but regardless, stemware was rarely signed. This numbering system appears to have been used by all members of the Afors group, therefore a piece signed "Boda" would have the 5 digit numbering system, as would one signed "Boda-Afors" or "Kosta Boda."

Sometime between 1984 and 1986, the signatures became uniform regardless of the factory in which they were produced (Afors, Boda, or Kosta) and had both the artist name and the "Kosta Boda" name. By 2002, Kosta Boda changed the numbering system again to include a 7 digit system, rather than a 5 digit system. Now the first 3 digits indicate the type of ware, while the fourth and fifth digit indicate the year of design. Web site: www.kostaboda.com

Artists at Kosta (with known designer codes):

Note that current designers working at Kosta, together with current designers at Afors and Boda, comprise the design team at Kosta Boda.

Axel Enoch Borman	1895-1903
Gunnar Wennerberg	1989-1902; 1908
Kai Neilsen	1903-1904
Ferdinand Boberg	1905
Karl Lindeberg	1907-1931
Alf Wallander	1908-1909
Edvin Ollers (O,F)	1917-1918; 1931-1932
Karl Hulstrom	1917-1919; 1927-1928
Lennart Nyblom	1919

Sten Branzell	1922-1930
Sven Erixson & Arnold Karlstrom	1923
Sven Erixson	1929-1931
Ewald Dahlskog	1926-1929
Sven Philstrom	1926-1969
Einar Nerman	ca. 1926
Elis Bergh (BH)	1929-1950
Sven-Erik Skawonius	1933-1935; 1944-1950
Tyra Lundgren	1925
R.A. Hickman	1937
Oskar Dahl	1939-1940; 1942-1944
John Kandall	1946
Vicke Lindstrand (L)	1950-1973
Ernest Gordon	1953-1955
Mona Morales-Schildt (SS)	1958-1970
Ann Warff	1964-1978
Goran Warff	1964-
Stig Lindberg	1965
Rolf Sinnemark	1967-1986
Sigurd Persson	1968-1982
Lisa Bauer	1969-1991
Paul Hoff	1972-1982
Hertha Hollfon	1974
Anna Ehrner	1974-
Bengt Edenfalk	1978-1989
Klas-Goran Tinback	1976-1981
Max Walter Svanberg	1980
Harald Wiberg	1980
Bengt Lindstrom	1982
Gun Lindblad	1982-1987
Christian von Sydow	1984-1989
Gunnel Sahlin	1986-
Ann Wahlstrom	1986-
Anne Nilsson	2001-

Kumela

Kumela Glassworks was founded in Riihimaki in 1933 by Finnish glass painter Toivo Kumen, who later changed his surname to Kumela. In the beginning, Kumela was just a small studio with four workers; the three Kumela brothers, Toivo, Ilmari and Oiva, and one hired worker. They specialized in enamel glass painting, engraving, and cutting. The founder's idea was just to streamline operations for other Finnish factories such as Riihimaen Lasi. However, the business idea was successful and after three years of activity, the Kumela brothers decided to build a factory. At the end on 1936, corporate form changed from sole trader to family-owned company with the name Osakeyhtio Kumela (Oy Kumela). Construction for the new factory started in the summer of 1937 and production started in the autumn of the same year. The new factory produced mainly household glass and art glass.

In 1937, Oy Kumela employed 40 workers and the number of workers increased to over 150 by 1948. During the Finnish Winter War (1939-1940), production at the Kumela Glassworks was interrupted for a few months. During the late 1940s and early 1950s, Oy Kumela mainly produced bottles for the pharmaceutical and food industry, but the company also produced glass lamp shades, utility glass for restaurants and mass-catering use, household glass, and art glass. In the mid-1950s, in order to increase production, machine made glass needed to be made and more capital was needed.

Because of continuous competition in both foreign and domestic markets, the company was forced to reduce its range of products. In 1960 the machine made bottle production became unprofitable and the production ended, and the factory concentrated in hand blown objects again. At that time, Kumela had returned to its beginning: glass painting, cutting and engraving, but now those styles had fallen out of favor and wares did not sell well. In the beginning of 1970s Kumela had to close its glass cutting and engraving departments and the energy crisis forced the owners to sell the company to Humppila Glassworks in 1976. At that time, the name was changed to Kumelan Lasitehdas Oy.

After 1977, the new owner started to modernize the production process at the factory, and bought new machinery and equipment to manufacture high quality tableware and art glass gift wares. Production resumed in 1979, and part of it was based on traditional middle-European crystal designs, and another part based on modern Finnish design. The idea was to develop and design specialty glass for export, however this was not fruitful, and, in 1980, Kumelan Lasitehdas Oy closed.

In the beginning, the brothers Toivo Kumela and Ilmari Kumela were the main designers in glass enameling and engraving. Toivo Karjalainen (1937-1976) was also a designer in the 1930s. Another designer during the 1940s was Sulo Gronberg (1940, 1947-1969). Designers during the 1950s include Maija Carlson (beginning in 1950), Sirkku Kumela-Lehtonen (1955-1976), Eero Sallinen (1956-1968) and Italian master glass blower, Armando Jacobino (1959-1970), who is probably the most important and best known Kumela designer. He came to the company after his employment at Nuutajarvi Notsjo, which ended in 1958. Jacobino's training as a glassblower is often expressed in the technically difficult art glass pieces he designed for the company.

During the 1970s, an important designer in the company was Kai Blomqvist (1968-1976), who created some colorful, ice-like "Kallo" (rock) vases, which resemble the work of Timo Sarpaneva and Tapio Wirkkala for iittala. Pentti Sarpaneva (1969-1978) also worked for Kumela during the 1970s. He created geometric vases, which incorporated the use of metal lace in the design. Other designers during the years were Ulla Kraemer, interior architect Olavi Ruottinen, Veikko Pekkola, Martti Helenius, Runar Engblom, Jyrki Sailo, Eero Sallinen, Sulo Tommila, Hillevi Lalla (1977) and Pertii Piipponen (1978-1981).

Lindshammar

The company was founded in Sweden in 1905 by Robert Rentsch, a German glass blower who previously worked for Kosta and Pukeberg. In 1916, the company was acquired by Anton Petersson, who modernized the factory and included a new blowing room. In 1949 Petersson's son, Erik Hovhammar assumed control and completely rebuilt the factory. Bankruptcy was declared in 1981 and the company was sold in 1984 to Ulf Rosen. In 1998 the Norwegian group CG Holding bought Lindshammar. This holding company also owns Hadeland in Norway. Since 2001, part of Lindshammar´s product is marketed under the trademark Steninge Slott. Lindshammar continues to produce glass today.

Primary production in the early years was cut glass tableware and colored ornamental wares, mainly for export. During the Second World War, production also included preserving jars and bottles. In 1949, the company began producing art glass and employed artist Gunnar Ander, who remained at the company until 1979.

Other artists were hired after him, including Christer Sjogren (1963-present), Tom Moller (67-89), Gosta Sigvard (1965-1980, born 1939), Sigvard Bernadotte (1970s), Catharina Aselius-Lidbeck (70-89), and Matz Borgstrom (90-92).Erik Hoglund worked freelance at the company from 1978 to 1981.

Production on blown glass declined during the 1970s and molded and centrifuge glass became the main production. In 1984, Ulf Rosen began reintroducing blown glass, both as art glass and everyday, functional items. The current designers at the factory include Lillemor Bokstrom, Bosse Falk (since 2000), Maud Gjeruldsen Bugge, Lena Hansson, James Hamilton (since 1994), Britten Paag (since 1998), Jonas Torstensson (since 1986), Jan Wiberg, Lars Sestervik (since 1987), Mirjana Kos-Frithiof, Birgitta Watz and Sofia Wiberg. Web site: www.lindshammarglasbruk.se

Magnor

The glassworks was founded in Norway as early as 1896 in the deep forests near the Swedish border, just three kilometers from the border and 120 kilometers from Oslo. Today Magnor continues to produce hand blown glass. The factory currently employs 120 people, and also includes the Swedish company Johansfors, which was purchased by Magnor. Current production includes designs by Vebjorn Sand, Per Spook, Kathinka Dysthe, Johan Verde, Oivind Sand, Per Winge, Catherina Lande, Gro Eriksson, Stein Nilsen, Lars Carlson, Ewan Allinson, Maria Rud, Ardy Struwer, Astrid Gate, Helen Tapper, Monica Dulin, Sofia Bergman and Olav Froysnes.

Mats Jonasson Maleras

Maleras Glassworks was founded in 1924, in the Smaland region of Sweden, and specialized in tableware and art glass. During the 1930s, Maleras became a major supplier to the Swedish Cooperative Union and Wholesale Society. Architects from the union worked on designs for glass. Folke Walwing began at Maleras as an engraver in 1924 and was art director until 1970. Walwing designed cut, engraved, and pressed glass, and led a movement towards textured glass during the 1960s.

Mats Jonasson started working at Maleras in 1959 and left from 1969 until 1975 to work at Kosta. During the 1960s, Hannelore Oreutler, Ake Rojgard, and Anette Sviberg-Krahner designed for Maleras for short periods. Sviberg-Krahner returned to Maleras in the 1970s, joining Lisa Larsson and Marianne Westman. When Mats Jonasson returned, he began designing his own models and was made art director in 1981. From 1989 to 1991, Ingeborg Lundin, after winning acclaim for her designs at Orrefors, designed for Maleras. Maleras was incorporated into the Flygsfors group in 1965, and then joined the Royal Krona group in 1974. Kosta Boda took over the company in 1977. In 1981, Maleras Glassworks was purchased by its own employees and they ran the company.

In 1988, in order to fight off a take-over by Orrefors, Mats Jonasson bought enough shares to take control of the company. Since then, he has been the managing director, art director and chief designer. Currently he is joined by Erika Hoglund, since 1997, and Klas-Goran Tinback, since 2000, and Robert Ljubez, engraver and now designer. Together they make up the designing team at the company. All current art glass at the company is marketed under the name "Mats Jonasson Maleras". Web site: www.matsjonasson.com

Nuutajarvi (Nuutajarvi Notsjo)

Nuutajarvi is the oldest glass factory in Finland. The founders, Jacob Wilhelm de Pont and Harald Furuhjelm, began production in 1793 making primarily window glass, bottles, and household glass. The factory was modernized in 1851 and began producing pressed glass and filigree glass under the guidance of Charles Bredgem, a French glassblower. This led to Nuutajarvi becoming a company of note among Nordic glassworks.

In an effort to obtain designs of their own, Nuutajarvi held glass competitions in 1905 and 1906. After World War II, under the direction of Gunnel Nyman, Nuutajarvi became a force in the realm of the manufacture of art glass. The Stockholm Exhibition of 1946 was a breakthrough for Nyman's designs and she is credited for the creation of the Nuutajarvi's tradition of artists and glass makers working as teams in small glasshouses or cottages.

The factory burned down in 1950, but was rebuilt quickly and then sold to the Wartsila Group, which had also acquired Arabia. This union brought Kaj Franck to Nuutajarvi where he redesigned the company's utility glassware. Saara Hopea was appointed Kaj Franck's assistant in 1952 and she took on the task of redesigning Nuutajarvi's crystal. Franck had begun to use filigree glass techniques once again and together with Hopea, they forged a solid reputation for Nuutajarvi's utility glass, bringing simplified forms and a wealth of color to glass exhibitions, including the Milan Triennales of that period. Kaj Franck's work brought international acclaim in 1955 when he won the Lunning Prize.

The 1960s at Nuutajarvi brought renewed interest in high-quality pressed glass. Oiva Toikka was appointed designer in 1963 and Heikki Orvola came to Nuutajarvi in 1968. Toikka's bold use of color and sculptural techniques brought him attention and he received the Lunning Prize in 1970. Orvola used a mix of techniques in creating glassware, designing notable and unique pieces. Kerttu Nurminen came to Nuutajarvi in 1972. The popular "Mondo" glassware of 1988 was only one of the lines Nurminen designed. Markku Salo, another innovator of unique glass techniques, has been designing for Nuutajarvi since 1982.

Nuutajarvi celebrated its bicentennial anniversary in 1993. Art glass from the company has been marketed under the name "Pro Arte" since 1981 and the release of the first "Pro Arte" collection coincided with the bicentennial in 1993. iittala Oy Ab has owned Nuutajarvi since 1990 and most production moved to iittala, also owned by iittala Oy Ab, leaving Nuutajarvi to make only art glass. All of Nuutajarvi's glass is currently marked under the iittala name. However, the "Pro Arte" collection, which has been continued by iittala, still made a distinction between the art glass created at Nuutajarvi and the art glass created at iittala. Web site: www.iittala.com

Nuutajarvi's Staff and Freelance Designers and Artists:

Note that the current designers working at Nuutajarvi, together with the current designers working at iittala, comprise iittala's design team, and all wares are marketed under that name.

Gunnel Nyman	1946-1948
Kaj Franck	1950-1976,
	freelance 1977-1989
Saara Hopea-Untracht	1952-1959
Hilkka-Liisa Ahola	1950s
Vuokko Eskolin-Nurmesniemi	1956-1957

Harry Moilanen	1960-1962
Oiva Toikka	1963-1993,
	artistic advisor 1993-1998
Pertti Santalahti	1963,
	freelance 1969-1971,
	freelance 1982-
Heikki Orvola	1968-1983,
	freelance 1984-
Inkeri Toikka	1970-1992,
	freelance 1992-
Kerttu Nurminen	1972-
Aimo Okkolin	1978
Markku Salo	1983-1997,
	freelance 1997-
Taru Syrjanen	1988-1991
Tiina Nordstrom	1988-1990
Annaleena Hakatie	1993-
Sami Lahtinen	1995-
Harri Koskinen	1996-1998

Orrefors

In 1898 Johnan August Samuelson established the Orrefors glassworks on a property that also held a sawmill and iron foundry. In 1913, the glassworks and sawmill were acquired by Johan Eckman. Although his main interest was the lumber business, Eckman hired Albert Ahlin to manage the glassworks. A year before his death in 1819, Eckman acquired Sandvik glassworks and after his passing, his children ran both glassworks. In 1946, Henning Beyer purchased Orrefors and his family remained in charge until 1971 when an investment trust company called Incentive bought a majority of the company stock. The relationship between Incentive and Orrefors continued until 1994.

During the seventies Orrefors acquired Alsterfors, Flygsfors, Strombergshyttan, and Gullaskruf and all were closed in a few years. In 1990 Orrefors also acquired Kosta Boda. Currently Orrefors comprises the following companies: Orrefors, Sandvik, Kosta, Boda, Afors, and SEA. The earliest products from Orrefors were simple table glass, hollow ware, some cut and etched tableware, and sheet glass. Eckman and Ahlin were very interested in the future of art glass and hired Knut Bergqvist, a master glassblower, and Oscar Landas as chief gaffer, Heinrich Wollman, a glass painter, and Fritz Blomqvist to prepare designs. Simon Gate and Edward Hald were hired as designers in 1916 and 1917. To supplement the engraved glass production, Gustaf Abels joined the company in 1915.

In 1922, Orrefors opened the first school for glass engraving in Sweden. Sven Palmqvist and Nils Landberg attended the school and then designed for Orrefors and Sandvik for many years. John Selbing was also a designer but is most remembered for his photographs of glass. In 1928 Orrefors hired Vicke Lindstrand. Lindstrand's engraved optic bowls garnered much acclaim at the 1930 Stockholm Exhibition. Edvin Ohrstrom, who came to Orrefors in 1936, specialized in heavy monumental pieces. Ingeborg Lundin was hired in 1947 and Gunnar Cyren in 1959. The 1970s brought the retirement of many prominent designers, which paved the way for new designers such as Olle Alberius, Lars Hellsten, Eva Englund, Berit Johansson, and Jan Johansson. The new artists continued to develop new techniques and some also designed sculptural pieces for public spaces.

In 1987, Orrefors discontinued producing pieces from artists who were no longer active and allowed broader production of contemporary designs. Contemporary designers included Lena Bergstrom, Helen Krantz, Erika Lagerbielke, Anne Nilsson, Martti Rythonen, and Per B. Sundberg. In 1990 Orrefors bought and merged with Kosta Boda, becoming Orrefors Kosta Boda. In 1997, Orrefors Kosta Boda became part of The Royal Scandinavia Group.

Most of Orrefors pieces are signed and the signature and markings can include much information. The signatures are sometimes complex and at times confusing, because the company has changed the ways they signed their wares throughout the years. Here is some basic information about signatures that can be helpful for the collector in order to identify the designer and approximate year of production.

- The company name was signed first as "Orrefors" or "Of".
- The designer code follows, and it can be found in the following list of designers. Keep in mind that the designer code changed around 1970, and this can help identify if the piece is of earlier or later production than that year.
- The supplemental code follows. These supplemental codes were added in the 1930s, and some of the signatures around that decade or earlier might not include them. If lacking a supplemental code, the piece is likely engraved.

Some of these codes are:
A Cut glass
E Satin glass
F Cut overlay
I Painted glass
P Pressed glass
U Blown glass worked in the blowing room

- The production number follows. There are mainly 3 to 5 digits, and sometimes the last digit is separated slash (/).
- After the production number, some pieces were marked with a code designating the date but these can be difficult to understand as they are not simply a date, and are often difficult to read.

Artist	Years Employed	Designer Code (Pre-1970)	(Post-1970)
Heinrich Wollmann	1914-1923	HW	
Knut Bergqvist	1914-1928	KB	
Fritz Blomqvist	1915-1917	FB	
Gustaf Abels	1915-1959		
Simon Gate	1916-1945	G	SG
Eva Jancke Bjork	1915-1917		
Edward Hald	1917-1978	H	EH
Nils Landberg	1927-1972	N	NL
John Selbing	1927-1973	C/S	
Vicke Lindstrand	1928-1940	L	VL
Sven Palmqvist	1928-1971	P	SP
Flory Gate	1930		
Edvin Ohrstrom	1936-1957	F	EO
Fritz Kurz	1940-1946	KD	
Carl Fagerlund	1946-1980	R	
Ingeborg Lundin	1947-1971	D	IL
Gunnar Cyren	1959-1970, 1976-	B	GC

Jan Johansson	1969-	J	JJ
Styrbjorn Engstrom	1970		E
Henning Koppel	1971-1981	K	HK
Rolf Nilsson	1971-1972		
Olle Alberius	1971-1993	A	OA
Lars Hellsten	1972-	T	LH
Eva Englund	1974-1990	V	EE
Wiktor Berndt	1975-1979		
Owe Elven	1975-1978		W
Petr Mandl	1970s		
Borge Lindau	1970s		LL
Bo Lindekrantz	1970s		LL
Berit Johansson	1979-1983		BJ
Anette Krahner	1980-1981		AK
Arne Branzell	1980-1982		AB
Klas-Goran Tinback	1982-1983		KGT
Erika Lagerbielke	1982-		EL
Anne Nilsson	1982-2000		AN
Matz Borgstrom	1984-1990		MB
Helen Krantz	1988-		HZ
Vivianne Karlsson	1989-1993		VK
Lena Bergstrom	1994-		LB
Martti Rytkonen	1994-		MR
Per B. Sundberg	1994-		PS
Ingegerd Raman	1999-		
Malin Lindahl	2002-		
Gunilla Allard	2002-		

Plus Glasshytte

Plus Glasshytte was founded in 1958 in Fredrikstad, Norway by Per Tannum as part of a workshop cooperative. The cooperative workshops involve not only glass, but also ceramics and other types of art wares. Plus Glasshytte is the glass division. The glass workshop has been managed by Benny Motzfeldt since 1970. Most of Plus pieces are signed with an acid etched mark, but do not always identify the designer.

Pukeberg

Founded in 1871 in Pukeberg, Sweden, its early production was mostly pressed domestic glassware. The company was purchased in 1884 by Arvid Bohlmark and four years later became part of AB Bohlmarks Lampfabrik, producing lamps, lampshades, and items for oil lamps. Elis Bergh worked at the company from 1906 until 1915, followed by Harald Notini. The 1920s brought the production of fittings for electric lights. Pukeberg specialized for a time in large glass globes for advertising signs for gas stations and garages.

Decorative glass production started in the 1930s. Uno Westerberg began designing light fixtures for the company and then turned to decorative glass wares in the 1950s. Westerberg worked at the company from 1935 to 1978. Goran Warff and Ann Wolff joined the company in 1958, met, married and stayed until 1964. Eva Englund came in 1964 and left the company by 1973, but returned after 1989. Together, the Warffs and Englund revitalized Pukeberg with new designs for art glass.

However, Pukeberg had serious financial difficulties during the 1980s. In 1998 the company was purchased by the Nolendorf and Gil families, who also own Zero Interior AB (lighting) and Lustrum (furniture). Erik Hoglund worked freelance at Pukeberg from 1978 to 1981. The 1970s also included designs by Staffan

Gellersted. During the 1980s the designers were Ginilla Lindhal, Carin Nordling, Lars Sestervik, Ragnhild Alexandersson and Ljupco Kocovski. During the 1990s the designers at the company were Eva Englund, Margreta Hennix, Liselotte Hendriksen, Borge Lindau, Rolf Sinnemark, Birgitta Watz and Carouschka Strejffert since 1996.

Most of the glass produced at Pukeberg was labeled and unsigned, although some of the more complex and sculptural pieces were signed.

Randsfjord Glassworks (Randsfjordglass)

Randsfjord Glassworks was founded in 1948 at Jevnaker in Norway. Initial production consisted mostly of utilitarian and functional glass for homes. In its early years, Randsfjord had about 50 employees. By 1951, the factory was consumed by a fire and had to be rebuilt. During this second phase of production, the company continued to make tableware, but now also had to compete with cheap imports which were saturating the market.

The 1950s were difficult times, but the company managed to survive mainly by the ingenuity of their craftsmen, who now created the ideas for their wares. By 1967, the company wanted to go further with their production and for the first time hired a designer, Benny Motzfeldt, who previously had been employed by their competitor, Hadeland Glassworks. Motzfeldt infused the company with her inevitable art for experimentation, created some of the most exciting art glass pieces produced in Norway at the time. By 1970, she left the company and began working for Plus Glasshytte. At Plus, she worked closely with master glassblower Ragnar Pettersen, who had also previously worked at Randsfjord until 1964.

Besides Motzfeldt, numerous designers were employed by the company during the 1970s. Among them, Torbjorn Torgersen, Hanna Hellum and Ulla Mari Brantenberg are of notable importance. These designers continued to create highly experimental and visually exciting glass for the company, many with highly textural effects. In the 1980s, Randsfjord Glassworks was bought by their neighboring and competing company, Hadeland Glassworks. By the mid-1990s, production at the company ceased. Two noted young assistants worked at the glassworks prior to their closure: Vidar Koksvik and Kari Haakonsen. Now married, they run their own glass cottage, where they continue to design art glass. By the fall of 2005, they will have an exhibition of their work at the Natthagen Gallery in Loten, Norway.

Most of the glass produced at Randsfjord was labeled. In most instances, the label includes the designer. Some of their wares were also stamped "RG" during production. Although extremely rare, some hand signed pieces designed by Benny Motzfeldt and Torbjorn Torgersen have been found.

Reijmyre

The Reijmyre Glassworks was founded in 1810, by Johan Jacob Graver in Reijmyra, Ostergotland, Sweden. Initial production consisted of engraved and pressed tableware and art glass. By 1900, the company had become a leader in the industry. In 1908, Alf Wallander and Axel Enoch Bowman joined the company and designed glass in Art Noveau styles. Monica Bratt was the design director for the company from 1937 to 1958.

In 1958, Paul Kedelv began working for Reijmyre and continued designing organic and free-flowing forms similar to those designed at Flygsfors, such as the "Harlequin" vases designed in 1958. During the 1960s, Tom Moller and Tyra Lundgren were employed as designers. In 1978, the company was acquired by the Upsala-Ekeby concern.

Riihimaen Lasi (Riihimaki)

The Riihimaki Joint Stock Company was founded in Riihimaki, Finland, by M.A. Kolehmainen and H.G. Paloheimo in 1910 and renamed Riihimaen Lasi in 1937. Riihimaki manufactured household glass, container glass, crystal, window glass, and eyeglass lenses and was Finland's largest glass factory from the 1920s to the 1960s. The company underwent modernization from 1927 to 1948, under the direction of Roope Kolihmainen.

Work was commissioned from designers like Tyra Lundgren and Eva Gylden from the 1920s on. In 1928 Henry Ericsson, who had won a glass design competition open to the public, was hired. Orrefors was dominating the glass export trade at that time and Riihimaki took aim at that market. Ericsson asked Gunnel Nyman to design for Riihimaki in the early 1930s and she made both glassware and art glass.

Reaching out with glass competitions in 1933 and 1936, Riihimaki began design associations with Arttu Brummer and Aino and Alvar Aalto. The company engaged a host of designers including Elis Muona, Antii Salmenlinna, Gunnar Finne, Yrjo Rosola, Greta-Lisa Jaderholm-Snellman, and Elmar Grunland. Glass cutter and later designer Aimo Okkolin was hired in 1937. The designer Helena Tynell was hired in 1946. At a Nordic glass competition in 1949, Arttu Brummer took first place, Timo Sarpaneva won second place, and Helena Tynell took third. Nanny Still was hired in 1949. From 1968 to 1985, E.T. (Erkkitapio) Siiroinen was employed at the company.

Riihimaki began a cooperative agreement with A. Ahlstrom in 1961 and manual production of glass ended in 1976 when the company turned to mass production. Household glass was also produced in 1977 by the newly founded Kotilasi unit. A. Ahlstrom bought Riihimaen Lasi in 1985 and in 1988 was it merged with Karhula to form Ahlstrom Riihimaen Lasi Oy. Riihimaen Lasi closed in 1990 and in 1995 Owens-Illinois, an American company, bought Karhula.

Riihimaki Glass Staff and Freelance Designers and Artists:

Tyra Lundgren	1920s
Eva Gylden	1920s
Theodor Kappi	1925-1939
Henry Ericsson	1928-1933
Arttu Brummer	1933-1951
Gunnel Nyman	1932-1947
Aimo Okkolin	1937-1976
Greta-Lisa Jaderholm-Snellman	1937-1949
Helena Tynell	1946-1976
Nanny Still	1949-1976
Sakari Pykala	1954-1955
Tamara Aladin	1959-1976
E. T. Siiroinen	1968-1976, freelance 1976-1985
Eero Rislakki	1970s

Sea Glasbruk

Founded in 1956, Sea Glasbruk is located in the village of Kosta, in the region of Smaland, Sweden. From its inception, production has focused on decorative glassware and gift-ware, characterized by a clean and functional design. Current designers include Goran Anneborg, Lena Engman, Bjorn Ramel, Renate Stock and Rune Strand (until 2000). Still in production, Sea Glasbruk is now associated with Orrefors Kosta Boda Company. Web site: www.seaglasbruk.se

Skruf

The factory was founded in 1897 in the region of Smaland, Sweden by Robert Celander, who was previously the manager at Johansfors. In 1908 the company underwent bankruptcy and was reformed in 1910. In 1946, the facility was completely destroyed by a fire, but production resumed a year later. The 1960s brought modernization to the facility including equipment for the automated cutting and polishing of tableware. In 1974 Skruf joined the Royal Krona group, an enterprise which went bankrupt in 1977. The company was later purchased by Kosta Boda. In 1980, the company closed, but an independent group of glass blowers have continued to produce glass there from 1981 to the present. Skruf is now part of the Svenska Glasbruk Group in association with two other glass factories, Bergdala and Alghult.

Original production during the turn of the 19th century consisted mainly of simple drinking glasses and jam jars. Crystal glass was introduced after 1910. During the 1930s and 1940s, Skruf produced an extensive line of table and domestic glassware including some for export. Most of the pieces of this period were designed by Magni Magnusson, the chief gaffer. In 1953, Bengt Edenfalk joined the company as chief designer. During his time at the company, he designed numerous pieces of tableware, plain and cut, as well decorative art glass, both colored and transparent. Edenfalk left Skruf and moved to Kosta in 1978. Other designers associated with Skruf include Lars Hellsten (1964-1972), Ingegerd Raman (1981-1998), and Annete Krahner (1982-1994).

Strombergshyttan

Founded in 1876 in Sweden as the Lindfors glassworks, production consisted of plain, cut, engraved, painted, and pressed glassware for homes and restaurants. The company was purchased by the former head of Orrefors, Edward Stromberg, in 1933. He changed the company name. Working with his son, Eric, Edward Stromberg experimented until they produced glass with a bluish silver hue, a color which became the factory's specialty. Using this new glass, Gerda Stromberg designed glass which was executed by glassblower Knut Bergqvist from 1933 to 1955. Asta Stromberg also worked as a designer for the company from the late 1930s until 1976. Eric Stromberg purchased the company after his father's death in 1945. After Eric died in 1960, his wife Asta Stromberg ran the company and modernized operations in 1962. Gunnar Nylund joined the design staff in 1952, staying until 1975. Rune Strand also designed for Strombergshyttan during the 1960s. There was a serious factory fire in 1973 which caused economic difficulties and the company was sold to Orrefors in 1976. Strombergshyttan closed in 1979.

Most of Strombergshyttan's wares were signed, although exceptions do apply; some pieces were only labeled. The signatures used were "Strombergshyttan" and "Stromberg" with a production code, but they were not designer specific. However, the production codes can provide information to help approximate the time the when pieces were designed. For plain vases, the production code consisted of the letter "B" followed by a series of numbers. For plain bowls, the production code consisted of the letter

"T" followed by a series of numbers. In the following list, the year of design is indicated in the upper horizontal column.

For example, a vase with a code of B936 was designed between 1954 and 1959/60. This becomes more complex when the pieces were engraved, because the engraving also has a design code, consisting of a letter and a series of numbers. It is important to remember that in engraved pieces the first code corresponds to the type and design of the ware and the second code corresponds to the engraving. It is also important to understand that Strombergshyttan produced more than just vases and bowls. Letters for other wares include "A" for plates, "E" for carafes and brandy glasses, and "O" for Liqueur bottles with glasses, to name a few.

Yr. of design	1935/36	1941	1944	1947	1954	1959/60	1962
Vases B	111	318	388	401	642	972	974
Bowls T	73	164	180	197	264	376	377

Studioglas Strombergshyttan

Studioglas Strombergshyttan is a hot glass studio where work can be done on a small scale and focus on the hands-on application of advanced glassblowing techniques. It was founded in 1987 by three master glassblowers, Mikael Axenbrant, Hakan Gunnarsson, and Leif Persson. At first it was a part-time venture, but soon the three men gave up their other jobs to work full-time at their new business.

Founders:

Mikael Axenbrant (b. 1957) "Hot glass must be treated like a woman — gently and with the utmost of care."

Hakan Gunnarsson (b. 1947) "Glass is an infinite source of surprise, often leading to new technical discoveries."

Leif Persson (b. 1941) "The warm soft glass has a life of its own — one has to realize this to work with the glass and not against it."

The three glassblowers have hosted guest designers including Erik Hoglund, Eva Englund, Bengt Edenfalk, and others. There are currently two in-house designers at Studioglas: Anna Ornberg (b. 1963), "I take everything that's funny very seriously.", "I want to make life more beautiful — and more fun."; and Ulla-Carin Bergqvist, "The whimsical nature of glass stirs my curiosity."

Transjo (Transjo Hytta AB)

Glass Studio established in 1978 at Transjo, near Kosta, under the name "Stenhytta" by Ann Warff and Wilke Adolfsson, a master glassblower formerly at Orrefors. The studio was to serve as a creative center for Swedish and international artists. Transjo Hytta AB was founded in 1982 by a group of glassblowers formerly at Kosta. The small factory produces art glass of exceptional quality, in limited quantities.

Designers

Aalto, Alvar (Kuortane, Finland, 1898-1976)

Hugo Alvar Henrik Aalto trained as an architect in the Helsinki University of Technology from 1916 to 1921. In 1933, he worked on a freelance basis with Riihimaen Lasi and designed the "Riihimaki flower," which won second prize in the Riihimaki design competition for domestic glassware of 1933. From 1932 to 1939, he did freelance work for Karhula, where he designed the "Savoy" vase (1936) and, in collaboration with Aino Aalto, the "Aalto Flower" (1939), which was first shown in the New York's World's Fair of 1939. In 1935, in collaboration with Aino Aalto and others, Alvar Aalto founded Artek, a Finnish furniture company, which featured many of Aalto's furniture designs.

Besides Alvar Aalto's significant design contributions in glass, furniture, and other areas, such as textiles, lighting and interior design, he will also be remembered as one of the most important architects of the 20th century. He was a practicing architect from 1923 until his death in 1976. Some of his most important architectural projects include the Viipuri Library (1927) and the Paimo Sanatorium (1929).

Aladin, Tamara (Finland, b. 1932)

Tamara Aladin worked at the ceramics factory, Arabia, from 1950 to 1951. She attended the Institute of Industrial Arts in Helsinki from 1951 to 1954. In 1959, she was hired as a glass designer for Riihimaen Lasi, where she remained until 1976. Her designs consist mostly of complex molded forms, many with colored underlays and textured surfaces, intended for mass production. Some of her designs for Riihimaen Lasi include the "Taalari" series (late 1960s), the "Kehra" series (early 1970s), and the "Safari" vases (early 1970s).

Most of Aladin's designs for Riihimaen Lasi were labeled, especially those produced in the 1960s and 1970s, however, some were also signed in this manner: Riihimaen Lasi O.Y. Tamara Aladin.

Ander, Gunnar (Sweden, b. 1908-1976)

Gunnar Ander graduated as an architect from the University of Handicrafts and Modern Design in Stockholm. From 1949 to 1976, he was employed at Lindshammar Glasbruk as a glass designer, and he was the first designer ever employed by the factory. Gunnar Ander designed numerous lines for the factory, including tableware as well as art glass, in almost any color imaginable.

His designs during the 1950s were geometric, but were often accentuated by surprising details to the designs, such as the subtle beveling of rims, or the bending of a decanter's neck. Many of his early designs were also engraved with lines which created geometric or curved patterns on the wares. One of Ander's designs, a conical decanter with an inverted teardrop stopper and a stamped application, was selected for the Corning Glass Museum's Special Exhibition of International Contemporary Glass in 1959 for its excellence of design.

During the 1960s and 1970s, Ander's designs became more organic and experimental and he explored the use of pigments to create internal patterns in the glass. During this time he also created some exceptional forms with heavily cased layers of glass in multiple colors, akin to the forms manufactured in Murano in the "sommerso" technique.

During the 1950s most of Lindshammar's wares were only labeled and not signed, but the labels identified the designer. However, by the 1960s and 1970s, many of Gunnar Ander's designs were signed in this manner: Lindshammar Sweden G. Ander, with the production number.

Backstrom, Monica (Sweden, b. 1939)

Monica Backstrom studied at The National College of Art Craft and design in Stockholm from 1959 to 1964. Since 1965, Backstrom has been a glass designer for Kosta Boda maintaining her studio at Boda Glassworks. In the beginning of her career at Boda, Backstrom, who was trained as a silversmith, experimented with the introduction of metal inclusions, crushed colored glass, fiber threads and foil, into the glass to create unique textures and unusual patterns.

She has continued to design in a forward and experimental fashion for Kosta Boda and has recently also created a line of wearable art glass for the firm. Some of her designs for Kosta Boda include the Zelda series (1975), a group of blown vessels with a satin surface with white and colored spots, and the "Terra" series (2003), a number of vessels with organic forms and earth-like coloration. Monica Backstrom and Erik Hoglund are the parents of Mats Jonasson Maleras glass designer, Erika Hoglund.

Bang, Jacob (Denmark, 1899-1965)

Jacob Bang received his education at the Royal Danish Academy of Fine Arts in Copenhagen from 1916 to 1921, and was trained as an architect. He worked for Holmegaard from 1927 until 1941, and was one of the few Danish artists working in glass during this period. He was appointed artistic director for the company in 1928. Together with Swedish engraver Elving Runemalm, Bang designed copper wheel engraved wares, some of the first to be designed in Denmark.

In 1941, he resigned from Holmegaard to concentrate in other artistic activities, including ceramics design. From 1943 to 1957, he was employed as artistic director for Nymolle Faience, a Danish ceramics company. In 1957, he returned to glass design, this time for Kastrup. He remained with the company until his death in 1965 and, just before the merger of Kastrup and Holmegaard. Jacob Bang created a large number of wares for Kastrup, including the "Opaline" series in 1960 and the "Capri" series in 1962.

Bang, Michael (Denmark, b. 1944)

The son of Jacob Bang, Michael trained as a ceramist at the Royal Porcelain factory (Royal Copenhagen) from 1964 to 1966, where he also designed. He was employed as a glass designer from 1966 to 1968 at Ekenas and at Holmegaard from 1968 to the present. In the beginning of his employment at Holmegaard, he was given specific commissions for the factory in Odense, which specialized in opaque glass. One of the results of this assignment was the "Pallet" series (1968), glassware in opaque white glass with strongly colored overlays.

Bergh, Elis (Sweden, 1881-1954)

Elis Bergh studied at the "Tekniska Skolan" and "Hogre Konstindustriella Skolan" (the schools of industrial art) in Stockholm. Bergh was employed from 1903 to 1904 in the office of Architect Agi Lindegren (architect of the Royal Castle). In 1905, he received a scholarship to study in Munich. From 1906 to 1915, he designed at the Bohlmarks lamp factory, designing many wares for Pukeberg. From 1916 to 1921, he worked at Herman Bergman's metal casting factory and from 1921 to 1928, he worked at Hallbergs Gudsmeds AB in Stockholm.

He was invited by Kosta to be their design director in 1929 and continued there until his retirement in 1950. Bergh's early design contributions to Kosta were mainly light fixtures, but he soon expanded his designs to include art glass and tableware. Many of his designs for Kosta involved cutting and engraving as well as the use of optics.

Bergslien (married name Sommerfeldt), Gro (Norway, b. 1940)

Gro Bergslien began her career studying textile design at the National College of Arts and Design in Oslo, where she graduated in 1960. In 1964 she graduated from the State School for teachers of drawing and woodwork. After working at the Plus cooperative in the textile group, she was employed at Hadeland in 1964, and has been associated with the glassworks ever since. Gro Bergslien's designs are characterized by an experimental technique, were glass chips of different colors are melded to produce painterly and abstract compositions.

Many of her designs are signed, but often in different ways such as: Hadeland Gro, Hadeland Gro Sommerfeldt, or Hadeland Gro B.S., with the production year, at times.

Bernadotte, Sigvard (Sweden, 1907-2002)

Prince Sigvard Bernadotte was the son of Swedish King Gustav VI Adolf and his wife Princess Margaretha, a granddaughter of Queen Victoria. He studied industrial design at The Academy of Fine Arts in Stockholm. Since the 1930s, he designed for the firm Georg Jensen and many of his designs in metal are still produced by the firm today. In 1934, marrying against his family's wishes, Bernadotte lost the title of Prince and was given the title of Count.

In 1949, Bernadotte went into partnership with the Danish architect Acton Bjorn and established the first Swedish drawing office for industrial design. This collaboration was extremely prolific and their designs can be found in most areas of Swedish culture. One of the most recognizable designs by Bernadotte is the "Margrethe" melamine bowls designed for the Danish firm Rosti in the 1950s. During the 1970s, Bernadotte designed a number of series in glass for Lindshammar Glasbruk.

Berndt, Wiktor (Sweden, b. 1919)

Wiktor Berndt studied at Kallstroms and then in Murano. He was a designer for Flygsfors from 1955 to 1974 and chief designer from 1956 to 1974. He designed light fixtures, but was also very involved in the production of art glass. During the late 1950s, Berndt designed some hand blown pieces with biomorphic forms and cut-out sections, with transparent colored glass combinations.

During the 1960s, he created some memorable mold-blown pieces with colored underlays and modernistic surface reliefs, often representing animals, people, or scenes. These surface reliefs were then ground, giving each piece unique hand-made characteristics. Berndt pieces for Flygsfors are often signed with his last name, the company name and the production year.

Blomberg, Kjell (Sweden, b. 1931)

Kjell Blomberg studied at Konstfack, the School of Arts, Crafts and Design. He was employed by Gullaskruf from 1954 to 1977. At least two of his designs, a decanter and beaker glasses in transparent gray glass, were selected for Corning Glass Museum Special Exhibition of International Contemporary Glass in 1959. Blomberg designs were often simple and geometric utility wares, but they struck the perfect balance between form and function, and resulted in beautifully designed and modern forms.

Although most of his wares for Gullaskruf were labeled, some pieces have been found with his signature.

Blomqvist, Kai (Finland b. 1931)

Kai Blomqvist studied at the Institute of Industrial Arts in Helsinki, concentrating in metal design. From 1958 to 1960, he worked at Georg Jensen in Copenhagen as a designer. From 1960 to 1965, he worked for the Finnish jewelry firm, Kultakeskus Oy, as a designer. From 1968 to 1976, he worked at Kumela as a glass designer and continued to work for Humppila after both glassworks merged in 1976. In 1988, Blomqvist continued to work in glass at iittala, as a freelance designer.

Blomqvist's most notable designs for Kumela include the "Kallio" (rock) vases, which were designed and produced from 1969 until the closing of the Kumela factory. These were highly textural forms in color, which resembled icy rocks, in a multitude of forms. For iittala, Blomqvist designed the "Silmu" clear glass candleholders in 1990.

Most of Blomqvist's designs for Kumela were signed in this manner: Kai Blomqvist Oy Kumela.

Borgstrom, Bo (Sweden, b. 1929)

Bo Borgstrom was the main glass designer with Aseda glassworks after 1955. He studied in Europe and America after training in Stockholm. During the 1960s, Borgstrom designed numerous wares for Aseda. His forms were often geometric and complex, and he widely explored the use of color in his designs. Many of his wares had underlays of colored glass, cased in clear as well as colored glass. During the 1960s he often used bright and distinctive opaque colors in his designs.

His designs for Aseda are mostly labeled and rarely signed.

Brauer, Otto

A Master Glass blower for Kastrup, Brauer is credited with designing Kastrup's famous "Gulvase," based on a Per Lutken design for Holmegaard. His gulvases were blown in colored transparent glass.

Bugge, Maud Gjeruldsen (Norway, b. 1962)

Maud Gjeruldsen Bugge studied at the Institute of Ceramics at the National College of the Arts in Norway. Since 1989, she has been a glass designer for Hadeland Glassworks and in 1994 became their Leader and Chief designer. Since the Norwegian group CG Holding bought Lindshammar Glassworks in 1998, she has been associated with Lindshammar as a designer.

Many of Bugge's designs for Hadeland are signed in this manner: Maud GJ Bugge Hadeland, with the year of design.

Edenfalk, Bengt (Karlskrona, Sweden, b. 1924)

Bengt Edenfalk studied art at Konstfack, the School of Arts, Crafts and Design in Stockholm, from 1947 to 1952. He worked at Skruf from 1953 to 1978 as chief designer and art director.

Upon his arrival at Skruf, most of the designs at the company consisted of utility ware. He began to design a whole new range of tableware that was suitable for cutting and engraving. He also designed art glass, which was unconventional and strikingly unique.

During the mid-1950s Edenfalk began exploring the use of trapped air bubbles created by manipulating the glass while still hot, and designed wares that had internal "air" decorations with primitive and unconventional anthropomorphic shapes. These experiments resulted in the "Thalatta" technique, which he often used at Skruf and throughout his designing career. He also created a series of vases and bowls with colored underlays and a thick layer of applied threading. The "Thalatta" vases, threaded vase, and other of his designs for Skruf were submitted to the Corning Glass Museum Special Exhibition of International Contemporary Glass in 1959. Of 4800 pieces submitted for this important exhibition, 15 were voted as "best in the world." Two of these were designed by Bengt Edenfalk.

In 1978, Edenfalk resigned as artistic director for Skruf and began to design for Kosta Boda, where he stayed until 1988. At Kosta Boda, he continued to design molded, blown, cut, and engraved pieces, and experimented widely with opaline glass and colored underlays in patchwork designs. Some examples of his designs for Kosta include the "Akvarellblock" (1986), a sculpture internally decorated with colored patches of opaline and transparent colored glass, and the "Claire de Lune" vase, an ovoid form in opaline white glass internally decorated blue opaline glass in different shades. Since 1989, Edenfalk has worked mostly on a freelance basis. He still continues to use the "Thalatta" technique extensively, now using multiple combinations of colored underlays.

Most of Bengt Edenfalk's designs for Skruf and Kosta Boda were signed, but exceptions do exist. Some pieces for Skruf that were only labeled might not identify him as the designer.

Ehrner, Anna (Stockholm, Sweden, b. 1948)

Anna Ehrner studied at the National College or Art, Craft and Design in Stockholm from 1968 to 1973. Since 1974, she has been employed as designer for Kosta and Kosta Boda. Her designs include "Line" (1981), one of Kosta Boda's most commercially successful designs, "Rock" (1991), "Woodlands" (2000), and "Wind" (2002).

Engman, Kjell (Stockholm, Sweden, b. 1946)

Kjell Engman studied at National College of Craft, Art and Design in Stockholm from 1973 to 1978. Since 1978, he has been a glass designer for Kosta Boda, maintaining his studio at Boda Glassworks. He is a highly prolific designer, and his designs account for a fifth of Kosta Boda's catalog range.

Engman's designs range from simple yet stylized forms to highly conceptual and almost dream-like creations. His most complex designs have a surreal and often mythical quality to them. Some of his designs for Kosta Boda include the "Fidji" series (1988), a number of stylized vases in transparent colored glass and the "Well..." animal sculptures (2001), a series of anthropomorphic statues with animal heads.

Most of Kjell Engman's designs for Kosta Boda are signed in this manner: K. Engman Kosta Boda, with a production number.

Engman, Lena (Sweden, b. 1959)

Lena Engman studied glass design at the Glass School at Kosta. Since 1995, she has been a glass designer for Sea Glasbruk. Besides glass design, she also enjoys working in photography, graphic art, painting and ceramics. Her designs for Sea Glasbruk are often hand-painted. Some of her designs for Sea Glasbruk include the "Birdie" series (1998), a number of vessels of bird-like forms with hand-painted decorations, and the "Swedish Summer" series, a number of opaque white vessels with hand-painted designs of flowers.

Franck, Kaj (Viipuri, Finland, 1911-1989)

Kaj Franck studied furniture design at the Institute of Industrial Art in Helsinki from 1929 to 1932. Franck is considered by many to be "the conscience of Finnish design." Functionality and compatibility were the underlying concepts of his streamlined utility articles, which he often chose to decorate only with color. He designed articles that were beautiful, functional, and affordable to the public.

His involvement in the design field was extensive. He was a glass designer for Riihimaen Lasi in 1934. From 1943 to 1973, he was the head of design of ceramic utility wares for Arabia and also design director from 1968 to 1973. He designed glass for iittala from 1946 to 1950. From 1950 to 1976 he was the art director for Nuutajarvi glass. Besides working in glass and ceramics, he also designed textiles, furniture, lighting and plastics.

In addition to glass utility wares, Franck also designed art glass which was often decorated with color, and also made simple colorless glass, many with internal bubbles. Some of his most notable designs include the "Teema" tableware (ceramics for Arabia designed in the 1950s and still produced), "Kartio" series (designed for Nuutajarvi Notsjo in the 1950s, now produced by iittala), "Soap Bubble" vases (Nuutajarvi, 1951-1961), "Prisma" vases (Nuutajarvi, 1954-68), and "Kremlin Bell" decanters (Nuutajarvi, 1955-1960).

His awards at the Milan Triennales include a gold medal (1951), the Diplome d'Honneur (1954), the grand prix, and the Compasso d'Oro (1957). He also received the Lunning Prize (1955). His works are included in the following collections: the Victoria and Albert Museum, the Stedelijk Museum, Musée des Arts Decoratifs, the Museum of Modern Art, the Corning Glass Museum, the Cooper-Hewitt Museum, the Finnish Glass Museum, the Arabia Museum, the iittala Museum, and the Nuutajarvi Museum.

Kaj Franck.

Photo courtesy of iittala.

Gordon, Ernest (England, b. 1926)

Ernest Gordon graduated from the Royal College of Arts. In 1953, he joined Afors as a glass designer, and stayed until 1963. His designs where mainly simple organic forms with free-flowing lines, but he also explored designs with more sculptural lines.

Most of his designs for Afors were signed with his complete name or last name and also included his designer code, which was a "G," for Gordon.

Hakatie, Annaleena (Finland, b. 1965)

Annaleena Hakatie has designed for iittala since 1993, including the "Ballo" votive candle holder (1995), the "Kupla" series (1996) for the "Pro Arte" collection, and the "Hakatie" series (1998) for the "Relations" collection. She is also a visual artist whose artworks have been exhibited abroad and in Finland. She took part in the International Glass Biennial in Venice, 1998-1999. Hakatie lectures at the University of Arts and Design in Helsinki, from where she graduated as an industrial designer in 1995.

Hald, Edward (Sweden, 1883-1980)

Edward Hald received his artistic education at the Technical Academy of Dresden from 1904 to 1906, trained as a painter and architect, and, from 1908 to 1912, studied abroad, including Paris as a student of Henry Matisse. His career at Orrefors lasted from 1917 to 1944, and he was the managing director of the company from 1933 to 1944. He continued to work on a freelance basis until as late as 1978.

Some of his important early engraved pieces include the "Fireworks" bowl (1921) and the "Cactus exhibition" bowl and plate (1926). Hald also worked extensively with the "Graal" technique and in 1936 developed the "Fishgraal" series, which featured underwater scenes of fish swimming though seaweed. The "Fishgraal" vases were first produced in 1938.

Hoglund, Erik Sylvester (Karlskrona, Sweden, 1932-1998)

Erik Hoglund is considered one of the most innovative glass designers of the 20th century. He studied sculpture at the National College of Art, Craft and Design in Stockholm from 1948 to 1953. In 1953 he began his career as a glass designer working for Boda and remained there until 1973. His main mission at that time was to create glass which would be sophisticated and easily recognizable as Boda. However, he managed to create distinct glass designs which were non-traditional and unique, and clearly departed from the Swedish aesthetic of the times.

His work at Boda ranged from the simple and almost rustic utilitarian wares to the highly decorated, but always primitive, engraved glass. Some of his techniques include the use of seed or bubbled glass, the addition of stamped or cast glass appliqués to blown forms and the use of free-hand engravings. He also mostly utilized colored glass rather than the most traditional clear glass. Although many artists see the material they work on as a form of inspiration, Erik Hoglund's inspiration was always free expression. He also used other materials such as metal while working at Boda, incorporating glass additions to such items as candleholders or candelabra.

In 1957, Hoglund received the prestigious Lunning prize for excellence in design. While Hoglund continued with his position as chief designer at Boda, he married Monica Backstrom, a designer who came to Boda in 1964. Their daughter, Erika Hoglund, is currently a designer at Mats Jonasson Maleras.

After he left Boda in 1973, Hoglund established his own studio, and mostly created sculptures. In that same year, he also taught glass design at the Pilchuck Glass Center in Washington State. From 1978 to 1981, he returned to glass design by working on a freelance basis with both Lindshammar and Pukeberg. Erik Hoglund passed away in 1998.

Many of Hoglund's designs for Boda were signed, but only with an H and the production numbers, without reference to the Boda factory. Most of his elaborate art glass pieces for the company are signed with his last name, a production number and the Boda name.

Hoglund, Erika (Sweden, b. 1971)

Erika Hoglund was raised in a family of artists in Smaland, Sweden. Both her father, Erik Hoglund, and her mother, Monica Backstrom, are well known and important glass artists. Erika studied at Parsons Institute, the art school in New York City. After her studies, Hoglund went to Mexico and Guatemala, where she decided to settle down for a while as a local. Her experience there was a fruitful one. It enabled her to eventually bring back to Sweden a broader understanding in culture, the arts, and life in general.

Despite the rich knowledge she gained through her travels, the impressions she received during her stay abroad were not the inspiration behind her first collection, "Artemiss." Instead, her source was old Swedish mythology, "Huldran." The forms found in the "Artemiss" series, resemble sensual females figures encapsulated in clear glass, many hand-painted with complex patterns and designs. Since 1997 she has been a designer for Mats Jonasson Maleras.

Holmgren, Christer (Sweden)

Christer Holmgren was employed as glass designer for Holmegaard from 1957 to 1972. His tableware designs include "Icepole" and "Iceflame," both with heavily textured surfaces. In the latter years at Holmegaard, he also worked in conjunction with his wife, Christel Holmgren, and they designed the "Blue Hour" line collaboratively.

Christer Holmgren designs are usually signed with a "C" in conjunction with the Holmegaard name and the design number.

Hongell, Goran (Finland, 1902-1973)

Goran Hongell studied decorative art at Central School of Industrial Design and taught decorative painting in later years. He was employed at Karhula from 1932 until his retirement in 1957. Many of his early designs were simple pieces in clear, blue, and green transparent glass, which were engraved and cut with scenes of Finnish provincial everyday life. He is considered one was one of the pioneers of the Finnish glass tradition. As far back as the 1930s, he presented the first version of what would become his most famous creation, the "Aarne" glassware set (1948). It was this very glassware that won the gold medal at the 1954 Milan Triennale. His "Aarne" glassware was selected as the symbol of the iittala glassworks for its centennial in 1981.

Hopea-Untracht, Saara (Porvoo, Finland, 1925-1984)

Saara Hopea studied industrial design at Central School of Industrial Arts from 1943 to 1946. She began her career designing furniture for Majander Oy from 1946 to 1948. From 1948 to 1952, she worked as a designer of lighting fixtures for Taito Oy.

From 1952 to 1959, she was employed as a designer and assistant to Kaj Franck at Nuutajarvi Notsjo and Arabia, where she designed ceramics, utility glass and art glass. Her utility glass was characterized by streamlined, geometric forms which were very appealing for everyday use. One of her most notable designs of tableware was a series of stacking glasses with widened rims in various colors which she created in 1952. This design won a silver medal at the Milan Triennale in 1954. In that same year, she designed one of the most recognizable forms in Scandinavian art glass, the "Pantteri" (Panther) vase. This vase consisted of a slightly globular cylindrical form, with spots in either green or purple glass and trapped air bubbles. The "Pantteri" vase exemplifies the economy of design which was a prevalent and desired production idea during the 1950s in Finland.

After working at Nuutajarvi and Arabia, Saara Hopea continued to design objects such as jewelry. In 1960 she married American enamellist and writer Oppi Untracht, who was associated with the publication "Craft Horizons". She also took to designing enameled metals, and some of her designs are in the collection of the Museum of Modern Art in New York.

Many of her designs for Nuutajarvi Notsjo are signed in either of these manners: SH Nuutajarvi Notsjo, or S. Hopea Nuutajarvi Notsjo-55 (year of production, for example).

Hydman-Vallien, Ulrica (Stockholm, Sweden, b. 1938)

Ulrica Hydman-Vallien studied at the National College of Art, Craft and Design in Stockholm, Sweden from 1958 to 1961. In 1963, she married glass designer and sculptor, Bertil Vallien. In the early 1960s she worked and traveled throughout the United States and Mexico, but by 1964 returned to Sweden and established her ceramics studio at Afors.

In 1972, she began working for Kosta Boda and has been a glass designer for the company ever since. Hydman-Vallien has not only worked in glass and ceramics, but has explored design in different media, such as textiles, paper design, illustration and industrial design, among others. From 1984 to 1986, she designed porcelain for the Swedish ceramics firm, Rorstrand. In 1990, she began working as a textiles designer for Kinnasand Textil AB. In 1997, she began working for British Airways and designed the colorful tail decorations on the BA 5 aircrafts.

In her designs in glass for Kosta Boda, Ulrica Hydman-Vallien has worked extensively in hand-painted decoration, but not exclusively. Her hand-painted designs are often characterized by human, animal, and flower forms, with an underlying emotional component expressed though the creative use of color and composition. Her hand-painted glass designs for the firm have been very commercially successful and include the series, "Caramba" (1987) and "Open Minds" (1987).

Most of Ulrica Hydman-Vallien's designs are signed, often by the use of her initials "UHV" in painted glass, or her name and last name initials, "Ulrica HV". Designs that are not hand painted are often signed on the bottom in this manner: Kosta Boda Ulrica HV, with the design number.

Jacobino, Armando (Italy, 1922-1970)

Armando Jacobino traveled to Finland and was employed as master glassblower for Nuutajarvi Notsjo from 1951 to 1959. During his employment at the firm, he also designed some pieces offered in the catalogs, which where mainly figurals. From 1959 to 1970, Jacobino was employed at Kumela as a glass blower and glass designer, and he continued to create figurals as well as art glass pieces. Many of his designs were cased with underlays, sometimes in opaque glass as well as colored transparent glass. He also used internal elongated air bubbles in his designs, reminiscent of the technique used by Kaj Frank at Nuutajarvi during Jacobino's tenure at the firm.

Many of his pieces were signed "Oy Kumela Jacobino" or "Oy Kumela A Jacobino."

Johansson, Willy (Norway, b. 1921)

Willy Johansson was working for Hadeland in 1936 at the age of 15, in the glass making workshop. From 1939 to 1942, he trained at the State School of Applied Art and Crafts in Oslo. He then returned to Hadeland where he was employed from 1946 as a full designer. He was awarded a gold medal in the Milan Triennale of 1957. His work is represented in many Scandinavian museums and in America at the Corning Museum of Glass.

Many of Johansson's wares for Hadeland were signed, usually with his initials, "WJ", the company name and at times the year of production or production number.

Jonasson, Mats (Sweden, b. 1945)

Mats Jonasson started at Maleras in 1959 upon leaving school at the age of fourteen. The glass works needed an engraver and, since Mats was known to be good at drawing, his father, who was employed there, was asked if his son could start as an apprentice. After some ten years at Maleras, Jonasson moved to Kosta in 1969, working as a designer, but returned to Maleras in 1975, also as a designer. Since 1988 he has been the managing director for the company.

Jonasson is a master engraver as well as a designer. His designs include molded and engraved crystal relief sculptures, such as the "Wildlife" series, which includes numerous life-like depictions of animals in the wild, and "Nordic Birds," which depicts the wild birds of the Scandinavian region. He also created a series of sculptures such as "Man's Best Friend," in which he depicts domestic animals. Recently he has also introduced the "Totem" series and "Masq", a group of figural sculptures, some resembling primitive and tribal masks.

Arne Jon Jutrem (Finland, b. 1929)

Arne Jon Jutrem studied at the National College of Art and design in Oslo from 1946 to 1950. In 1952, he attended Fernand Leger's Academy in Paris. From 1950 until 1957, he worked as a designer on applied arts, including electronics. During this period, he also designed furniture, textiles, pewter, books and posters. From 1950 to 1962, he was employed as a glass designer for Hadeland Glassworks., where he designed both utilitarian products and art glass. From 1962 to 1964 Jutrem worked for Holmegaard Glassworks in Denmark on a freelance basis. In 1967, he worked for Plus Glasshytte. In 1985, Jutrem was again at Hadeland and was appointed art director of the company. Arne Jon Jutrem was awarded the prestigious Lunning Prize in 1959, for excellence in the field of design and also won a gold medal at the Milan Triennale of 1954.

Many of the pieces Jutrem created for Hadeland were signed with his initials, AJJ, with the company name and year of production.

Kedelv, Paul (Sweden, b. 1917)

Paul Kedelv worked for Orrefors from 1937 to 1946, before receiving his education at the National College of Art, Craft and design in Stockholm, where he was taught by Edvin Ohrstrom. In 1948 he worked for Nuutajarvi Notsjo, before he began working at Flygsfors in 1949. He remained at Flygsfors until 1956.

During his tenure at Flygsfors, Kedelv created the most recognizable ranges of art glass ever manufactured at the company. The "Coquille" range was produced in 1952, and it continued to be produced into the late 1960s, even after Kedelv had left the firm. The "coquille" range is characterized by organic forms with cased layers of transparent and opaque colored glass, which were inspired by sea shells. Kedelv also created the "Flamingo" series, which consisted of forms in clear glass, internally decorated by numerous strands of colored glass, in a seemingly haphazard fashion.

After Kedelv left Flygsfors, he joined the team of designers at Reijmyre, where he remained until 1978. During his tenure at Reijmyre, Kedelv created the "Harlequin" vases around 1958. These vases resembled the "Coquille" range and were cased in layers of different colors, and were often in pulled, bone-like forms.

Kedelv's pieces for Flygsfors were often signed, mostly by the range that they belonged to, as well as the date and the company name. Some pieces were also signed with his last name, without identifying the range. The signatures and identification for the Reijmyre pieces is more difficult as they usually used only letters and numbers for the year of production and production number. For example, some of the "Harlequin" vases were signed in this manner: R-e-58 (R-e stands for Reijmyre, 58 is the year of production) K-18(K stands for Kedelv and 18 is the production number).

Lake, John-Orwar (Sweden, b. 1921)

After training in Stockholm, partly as a sculptor, John-Orwar Lake joined Arabia in Finland to do some ceramic work. He then returned to Ekenas in Sweden in 1953, and was the chief designer also in charge of product development until 1976. Lake was a talented glass designer. His early designs in the 1950s were mainly intricately engraved and cut pieces in clear glass of exceptional quality. During the 1960s, he continued designing cut and engraved glass, but also experimented and created some organic forms in which he explored color, texture, and internal decoration, not unlike the art glass being created in the USA during the studio glass movement in the 1960s.

Most of his designs were signed, although some, especially his earlier ones were labeled and unsigned.

Koskinen, Harri (Karstula, Finland, b. 1970)

Harri Koskinen was trained at the Lahti Design Institute from 1989 to 1993 and at the University of Art and Design UIAH, in Helsinki, Finland. In 1996, he worked as a designer for Nuutajarvi, and since 1998 has been employed at iittala. In 2002, he ventured into ceramic design with the "Air" containers with airtight plastic lids for Arabia. In his designs, Koskinen strives to arrive at new solutions that will be considered innovative by both the manufacturer and user. Koskinen's designs for iittala include the "Atlas" candle holder (1996), which was selected for the International Design Year Book, "Koskinen" candle lanterns (1999) from the Relations collection, "Klubi" barware (1998), and the "Muotka" vase (2000). In 2000 he won the Young Designer of the Year award, launched by Design Forum Finland and the Good Design prize, granted by Chicago Atheneum.

Landberg, Nils (Sweden, 1907-1991)

Landberg worked with Orrefors from 1925 to 1970. He attended the School of Arts and Crafts in Gothenburg, before joining Orrefors in 1925. For the first two years, he was in the Orrefors School of engraving, and in 1929 became the assistant to Edward Hald.

In 1936, he was given the title of full resident designer. His designs during the 1930s and the 1940s were mainly engraved pieces, many in transparent glass, but by the 1950s he had found his own sense of design. In 1954 he designed the "Tulip" glass series, a number of stylized forms with colored glass underlays and elongated stems. He was awarded the gold medal at the Milan Triennale in 1957 for this series. From 1954 to 1956, he also created some memorable designs which included heavily cased glass pieces, in organic forms, some with colored dark colored underlays, such as dark green, charcoal gray, and deep blue.

Lindfors, Stefan (Mariehamn, Finland, b. 1962)

Stefan Lindfors studied Interior Architecture and Furniture Design at the University of Art and Design in Helsinki, Finland, from 1982 to 1988. Since 2000, he has designed products for iittala, Arabia and Hackman, including the "Boy" (2000) series of glasses for iittala, and the "Ego" (2000) tableware for Arabia.

Lindfors has also worked for numerous companies in furniture, textile, graphic and industrial design. Lindfors is a prolific and multifaceted artist. He continues to design interior architecture and has also extensively created sculptures. Some of his sculptural work in the United States can be found at the Mercer Hotel in Soho, New York City, where he created a permanent sculpture for the lobby (1998), and at the Gershwin Hotel, New York City, where he created a sculptural installation for the façade of the hotel (1998). Lindfors has won several awards for excellence in design, including the Georg Jensen Award (1992), and the Good Design Award (1995) by the Chicago Atheneum.

Lindstrand, Vicke (Gothenburg, Sweden, 1904-1983)

Vicke Lindstrand studied at the School of the Swedish Society of Arts and Crafts in Gothenburg. He started to work for Orrefors 1928, where he worked closely with Simon Gate and Edward Hald. At Orrefors, Lindstrand created some of the most memorable engraved art glass pieces in Scandinavian design.

Although both Gate and Hald had often praised and used the nude female form as topic for their engravings, it was Lindstrand who began to use the male nude form as part of the decorations. During the 1930s, he created a series of vases with engraved underwater scenes of muscular male nude divers, which included "Pearl Fishers" (1931) and "Shark Killers" (1937), among others. He also explored the use of the "Graal" technique in the late 1930s, and created a "Graal" variation called "Mykene." It made use of carborudum powder, which when reheated, created a design of closely spaced air bubbles that still retained the original design form. While at Orrefors, Lindstrand also explored the use of surface cutting, but many times opted to leave unpolished areas to create a remarkable visual contrast with polished areas.

In 1940, he left Orrefors to design for Upsala-Ekeby ceramics company, and remained there until 1950. After leaving Upsala-Ekeby, he joined Kosta glass in 1950 and remained with them until 1972. While at Kosta, Lindstrand's design, powered by his untamed creativity, reached new heights. He continued to use engraving and cutting techniques, but also utilized color extensively, including internal colored decoration, sandblasting, and optics. His forms became much more organic, in concordance with the post-war tastes and changing times.

Lutken, Per (Denmark, 1916-1998)

Per Lutken trained in the School of Arts and Crafts in Copenhagen in 1937, mainly in painting and technical drawing. He was employed as artistic director for Holmegaard from 1942 until his death in 1998. Never having worked with glass before his employment at Holmegaard, Lutken experimented his way through the early years. His designs for Holmegaard were extensive. Some of the most famous ones include, the "Beak" or "Duckling" vase (1950), "Aristocrat" tableware (1956), "Cascade" vases (1970), and "Snowdrop" tableware (1978). Per Lutken is highly regarded as one of the most influential artists in Danish glass design and Scandinavian glass design as well.

The majority of the wares he designed were signed. He used different manners through the years, but often with his initials "PL" in conjunction with the company name and production number, or by themselves. However, some pieces were only labeled and unsigned.

Morales-Schildt, Mona (Sweden, 1908-1999)

Mona Morales-Schildt studied at the School of Industrial Art in Stockholm and won a scholarship to study ceramics in England and Germany. She also went to a painting school in Paris before starting to work for Gustavsberg in 1936 as an assistant to Willhelm Kage. In 1939, she worked for a year at Arabia. She then returned to Stockholm and managed the new Gustavsberg shop until 1941. After her marriage to the author Goran Schildt, she worked from 1945 to 1957 for Nordiska Kompaniet, the Stockholm department store, where she was responsible for all art exhibits.

In 1958 she joined Kosta and made her name with a very large range of glass designs. She is best known as the designer of the brightly colored and faceted pieces from the "Ventana" series (1961-1963), a range extending into vases and bowls with depth obtained by cutting through a range of warm colors.

Motzfeldt, Benny (Norway, b. 1909)

Benny Motzfeldt studied graphic design at the National College of Arts and Design. From 1955 to 1967, she worked as a designer at Hadeland. In 1967, she worked as a designer at Randsfjordglass. Since 1970, she has worked as a designer for the Plus Workshop and also managed their glass division, Plus Glasshytte.

During the 1970s, Benny Motzfeldt solidified her position as the most important Norwegian studio glass artist. Even when her designs were produced in larger numbers, they retained a certain uniqueness due to her intended treatment of the medium. She often explored the use of glass, metal, and gauze fiber inclusions in her designs, not necessarily or solely as decoration, but rather as an exploration of the reactionary quality of glass.

Her designs for Plus Glasshytte were often stamped with an acid etched mark reading "Plus BM Norway," while most of her unique pieces were simply engraved "BM" with the production year, for example "77."

Nordstrom, Tiina (Finland, b. 1957)

Tiina Nordstrom worked at iittala from 1988 to 1997, where she designed both utilitarian glass and art glass. Her designs are mostly influenced by the environment surrounding us and her inspiration comes from nature, architecture, history and culture. Some of her designs for iittala include the "Major" candleholders (1994), a series of egg-like vessels with sandblasted glass in different colors, and the "Leia" vases (1997), of ovoid flattened forms in clear glass.

Nurminen, Kerttu (Lahti, Finland, b. 1943)

Kerttu Nurminen studied at the Central School of Industrial design in Helsinki. Since 1972, she has been employed as a glass designer for Nuutajarvi. Her career continues to this day with the same passion and unwillingness to compromise. Nurminen's talent first found international favor in 1988, when the "the great flame and fluid colors" of her "Mondo" glasses captured the limelight. Its method of manufacture and its unstinting originality exemplify Kerttu Nurminen's creative solutions. Her designs for Nuutajarvi and iittala include "Verna" tableware (1998), "Palazzo" filigree tableware (1998) for "Pro Arte," and "Lago" vases and bowls (2000) for "Pro Arte." She also continues to design unique pieces at Nuutajarvi, which often explore themes of nature and the beauty of the countryside.

In 1999, at an exhibition of her unique glass pieces, the artist pointed out that her works are mood pieces about nature, but not still lifes. Some of the names of the works shown in this exhibition were evocative of nature and its ever changing and inspirational palette: Paratiisi, Joki, Aiti maa, Karhutalvi (Paradise, River, Mother Earth, The Winter of the Bear).

Nylund, Gunnar (Sweden, b. 1904)

Gunnar Nylund studied architecture and worked as a ceramist at Saxbo, and at Bing and Grondahl in Copenhagen. He began his work at Strombergshyttan in 1953 and continued until 1967, both as glass designer and art director. From 1953 until 1957, he worked concurrently for Strombergshyttan and for Rorstrand, where he was the art director and ceramicist from 1931 to 1958. Also while working at Strombergshyttan, he was appointed art director at Nymolle Keramiske Fabriker in Denmark, serving from 1959 to 1974.

Gunnar Nylund's designs for Strombergshyttan are organic and sometimes sculptural, and easily distinguishable from those designed by Gerda and Asta Stromberg, which are mostly geometric, with very thick walls and polished rims. Nylund's designs were sometimes asymmetrical and organic forms with soft edges, and often included vibrant colored underlays cased in clear glass.

Although most of Strombergshyttan's pieces are signed, they rarely identify the designer.

Nyman, Gunnel (Finland, 1909-1948)

Gunnel Nyman was a pupil of Arttu Brummer and studied at the Central School of Industrial Design in Helsinki, graduating in 1932. She was employed at Riihimaen Lasi from 1932 to 1947. One of her notable designs at Riihimaen Lasi was the "Calla" vase (1946), with its form resembling the flower. She also worked for Karhula from 1935 to 1937, for iittala from 1946-1947, and for Nuutajarvi Notsjo from 1946 to 1948.

Nyman was one of the most influential designers in Scandinavian glass. Her ability to strike the perfect balance between form and function was remarkable. She often used minimal decoration such as controlled bubbles in simple organic forms, as well as in utility wares. From 1946 to 1948, while working at Nuutajarvi Notsjo, she reached the peak of her career, which was unfortunately cut short by illness and her subsequent death. Her designs for Nuutajarvi included the "Huntu" (Veil) vase, with an internal layer of controlled bubbles, the "Parlband" (String of Pearls) vase, with a single elliptical string of bubbles, and the "Serperntiini" (Serpentine) vase. Most of Nyman's designs for Nuutajarvi were signed in this manner: G. Nyman or GN, with the company name and the year of design. Wares of earlier production can be identified by an acid-etched signature, rather than an engraved one.

Ohrstrom, Edvin (Sweden, b. 1906)

Edvin Ohrstrom studied at the Stockholm Institute of Technology and the Stockholm Academy of Fine Arts, where he trained as a sculptor and graphic artist. From 1936 to 1958, he worked as a glass designer at Orrefors. During the mid-1930s, together with master glass blower, Gustaf Berqkvist, and Vicke Lindstrand, he is credited with the creation of the "Ariel" technique, which has been explored by many of the Orrefors artists since then. Besides his many creations using the "Ariel" technique, Ohrstrom also designed engraved and cut glass, especially one of Orrefors most commercially successful designs, "Wish to the Moon" (early 1940s).

Okkolin, Aimo (Finland, 1917-1982)

Aimo Okkolin is one of the main designers that worked at Riihimaen Lasi. He began working for the factory in 1937 as a cutter and engraver, but by the 1940s was designing utilitarian wares as well as art glass. Because of his training as a cutter and engraver, Okkolin managed to design some of the most intricate and technically difficult forms for the factory. Some of his most notable designs are the "Water Lilly" bowl (1960) , a heavily cut and faceted form resembling the pond flower, and the "Pack Ice" sculpture (1967), which was cut out of a block of lead crystal by Okkolin, and the "Majakka" (lighthouse) vase (1960s), a form which resembles a lighthouse shaped by intricate facet cuts. Okkolin also designed for Riihimaen Lasi pieces which were not cut or engraved.

His employment with Riihimaen Lasi ended in 1976. In 1977, he worked for the glass company Studiolasi Oy and for Nuutajarvi Notsjo in 1978.   Many of his designs, but not all, were signed in this manner: Aimo Okkolin Riihimaen Lasi Oy.

Orup, Bengt (Sweden, b. 1916)

Bengt Orup was trained as a painter in Paris from 1937 to 1938. From 1951 to 1973 he was a glass designer and then director at Johansfors. In 1963, he also worked on a freelance basis for Hyllinge Glasbruk. Some of his designs, including a decanter and beaker glasses decorated with black enameled stripes, were selected for the Corning Glass Museum Special Exhibition of International Contemporary Glass in 1959.

Orup is a master of design and form. During his tenure at Johansfors he explored the glass medium in every imaginable way. His work ranged from simple geometric forms to highly organic and asymmetrical forms. His designs ranged from simple tableware to sculptural pieces of art glass. As decoration, he utilized engravings, cuttings, inclusions in glass, as well as external applications. His use of color was also exceptional, sometimes simple and subdued, sometimes colorful and vibrant.

Orvola, Heikki (Helsinki, Finland, b. 1943)

Heikki Orvola trained in ceramics at the Central School of Industrial design in Helsinki from 1963 to 1968. He works with glass (Nuutajarvi and iittala, 1968-present), ceramics (Arabia, 1987-1993,and Rorstrand), cast iron, enamel and textiles (Marimekko,

1985-1995). Since 1994 he has been a freelance designer, and continues to work in any medium that sparks his attention.

For most of his career, Orvola has worked for industry, but for him artworks made of glass, ceramics, and textiles are a necessary outlet for his creative energies. A 15-year grant from the State, which he has received since the beginning of 1994, has increased his freedom to decide where to apply his energies. The Victoria and Albert Museum, the Museum of Modern Art, the Stedelijk Museum, the Finnish Glass Museum and the Arabia Museum are only some of the museums that have included Orvola's works in their collections.

During his career as an industrial designer, Orvola has received the Kaj Franck prize (1998), which is Finland's most important design award, and the Pro Finlandia medal (1984), among other awards. His designs for iittala and Nuutajarvi include the "Aurora" tableware (1972), "Vulcano" vases and bowls (1974-1977), "Filigraani" vessels (since 1980) for "Pro Arte," "Evergreen" vases (1996) and the "Kivi" candleholders (1998).

Many of Orvola's designs for Nuutajarvi were signed, usually with his complete name and company name.

Palmqvist, Sven (Sweden, 1906-1984)

From 1928 to 1930, Sven Palmqvist trained at the Orrefors Engraving School, as an apprentice under Edward Hald and Simon Gate. From 1931 to 1933 he studied at the Konstfack School of Arts, Crafts and Design in Stockholm, and then in the Royal Swedish Academy Art School from 1934 to 1936, training in sculpture. He also studied in Germany and Paris during the middle and late 1930s.

From 1936 to 1972, he was employed as a glass designer at Orrefors, but still did freelance work with the company after 1972 until his death in 1984. During the 1930s, 1940s and 1950s, Palmqvist worked with traditional techniques such as cutting and engraving, and created some magnificent and memorable pieces. Palmqvist is credited with developing the "Graal" technique into the styles known as "Kraka" (developed in 1944) and "Ravenna" (developed between 1948-1951). During the early 1950s, Palmqvist achieved great success with a line of domestic and functional wares in transparent glass known as "Fuga," which were ingeniously fashioned by centrifugal force. He used the same technique to create the "Colora" series, but these were made of opaque colored glass. For the "Fuga" series, Palmqvist was awarded the Grand Prix at the Milan Triennale of 1957.

Percy, Arthur (Sweden, 1886-1976)

Arthur Percy studied in Stockholm from 1905 to 1908, and in Paris in 1908. Besides being a glass designer, he was also a painter and ceramics and textile designer. In 1951, he joined Gullaskruf where he remained until 1965. His designs were mainly simple functional pieces, many mold-blown, but with exceptional attention to form. Some of his designs for Gullaskruf include the bottle vases (1952) and "Randi" bowls and vases (mid-1950s). Due to their excellence in design, some of Percy's wares for Gullaskruf, including his bottle vases, were selected for the Corning Glass Museum Special Exhibition of International Contemporary Glass in 1959.

Pors, Tora (Denmark)

Tora Pors was a Danish designer who studied under Isac Grunewald and professor Johansson-Thor. From 1947 to 1954, she worked as a glass designer for the Swedish factory, Kalmar Glasbruk, which was then run by Arnold Glave. She invented a technique she named "Myrica", which consisted of an internal decoration of the glass with a colored and linear design, sometimes in a pattern, sometimes in a haphazard arrangement.

Many of Tora Pos designs for Kalmar were signed in this manner: T. Pors Kalmar, with a production number.

Quistgaard, Jens Harold (Denmark, b. 1919)

Jens Quistgaard's early training was with his father Harold Quistgaard, a noted Professor of Sculpture at the Royal Danish Academy of Fine Arts. He later achieved his technical training as a designer, silversmith and potter. He completed his apprenticeship with Georg Jensen Silversmiths. In 1946, he became a free-lance designer with his own studio in Copenhagen working for, among others, De Forenede Jerstoberier for whom he designed enameled cast iron cooking pots which won him the Lunning Prize in 1954. Quistgaard started Dansk International Designs, Ltd., in 1954 with Ted Nierenberg, an American importer, and was its primary designer for the next 30 years. While at Dansk, Quistgaard designed objects and tableware in metal, wood, ceramics and glass.

Designs created by Quistgaard for Dansk, can be identified by his initials, "JHQ", or the letters "IHQ", on labels or marks.

Raman, Ingegerd (Sweden, b. 1943)

Ingegerd Raman graduated from the College of Arts, Crafts and Design in Stockholm in 1965. For many years, she worked as a ceramics designer and ran her own studio. She designed glass at Johansfors from 1968 to 1971 and was later employed at Skruf from 1981 to 1998. In 1999 she joined the team of artists at Orrefors. Ingegerd Raman has won the Excellent Swedish Design Award 17 times.

Many of Raman's designs for Johansfors are signed in this manner: Johansfors Raman.

Ramel, Bjorn (Gothenburg, Sweden, b. 1940)

Bjorn Ramel studied at the Gothenburg School of Arts and Crafts, at the School of Arts, Crafts and Design, at the National Swedish Institute for Trade and Industry and at the Pedagogical Institute. He has a studio located at Bergkvara and is considered one of Sweden's foremost wood sculptors. Since 1966, he has been a glass designer for Sea Glasbruk. Some of his series for Sea Glasbruk include the "Isbjorn" range (1998), a series of vessels in blue and white sandblasted glass, and the "Color" series, a number of candle holders and oil lamps in mottles green, blue and clear glass, which he designed in conjunction with Rune Strand in 1998.

Sahlin, Gunnel (Umea, Sweden, b. 1954)

Gunnel Sahlin studied at National College of Craft, Art and Design in Stockholm from 1980 to 1984. She has been a glass designer for Kosta Boda since 1986. In 1987, she studied at the Pilchuck Glass School Center in Washington State, US. Her designs in glass often exhibit subtle and refined exploration of form, color and texture. Some of her designs for Kosta Boda include the "Frutteria" series (1989-1993), a number of vessels in speckled glass and textured glass fruits, and the "Scribble" series (2004), globular vases in vivid colors with internal scribbles in the forms. From 1999 to 2004, Gunnel Sahlin was Professor of Ceramics and Glass at the National College of Craft, Art and Design.

Most of Gunnel Sahlin's designs for Kosta Boda are signed in this manner: G. Sahlin Kosta Boda, with a production number.

Salo, Markku (Nokia, Finland, b. 1954)

Markku Salo studied at the Helsinki University of Technology from 1974 to 1979. He is a bold and experimental glass artist. Salo began to work for Nuutajarvi in 1983 and continued to work for iittala after Nuutajarvi joined the Hackman group in the early 1990s. His designs are characterized by disciplined functionality and simple beauty.

His designs for iittala include the "Marius" glassware (1985), "Aava" vases (1998), "Nappi" candleholders (1998), and "Gabriel" candlesticks (1999). In 2001, Salo created some unusual glass bottles with wire legs resembling dogs for Nuutajarvi "Pro Arte." These dogs evolved from traditional predecessors: traditional "wine dogs" made by master glassblowers to show their skills, and also from Markku Salo's unique dog sculptures.

Salo's work also includes graphic design, ceramics design at Arabia, and electronics design. He has his own studio at Nuutajarvi, where he has created glass sculptures and installations for the Malmi House in Helsinki and the Strand-Intercontinental Hotel. Salo's works are featured in the collections of the Corning Museum of Glass, the Cooper-Hewitt Museum, the Victoria and Albert Museum, Glasmuseum Ebeltoft, the Finnish Glass Museum, and the Arabia Museum, among others. His work has been recognized with the Georg Jensen Award (1990) and the State's Industrial Arts Award (1989).

Santalahti, Pertti (Finland, b. 1941)

Pertti Santalahti studied at the Institute of Industrial Arts in Helsinki from 1959 to 1962, concentrating in sculpture. In 1962, he worked as a designer at the ceramics factory in Finland, Kupittaan Savi. In 1963, he worked as a glass designer for Nuutajarvi. From 1964 to 1966, he worked as an art teacher, while also designing glass for Alsterfors in Sweden. In 1968, he was employed as a ceramics designer at Arabia. From 1969 to 1961, he worked on a free-lance basis at Nuutajarvi, designing glass. From 1971 to 1981, Santalahti was employed as a full-time glass designer for Humppila Glassworks.

Since 1982, he has continued working as a freelance designer for Humppila, Nuutajarvi, and iittala. Santalahti's work for Humppila consisted of some highly textural, cast forms, with blending of colors. One of his most recognizable series is "Kasvimaalla" (vegetable garden), which he designed in the mid-1970s and consisted of floral and vegetable-like cast forms.

Many, although not all of Pertti Santalahti designs for Humppila were signed in this manner: Pertti Santalahti Humppila Finland. Some of his early designs for Nuutajarvi were signed with his initials- PS.

Sarpaneva, Pentti (Finland, 1925-1978)

Pentti Sarpaneva studied graphic design at the Institute of Industrial Arts in Helsinki. He was part of a very artistic family and Timo Sarpaneva was his younger brother. During his thirties, he began designing jewelry and was a designer for the Finnish company Kalevala Kuru, as well as Turun Hopea during the 1960s and 1970s. His work in metal was mostly cast and many of his designs resembled finely crafted lace. Sarpaneva incorporated his metal designs to the glass pieces he created for Kumela Glassworks from around 1969 until 1978.

Many of his designs for Kumela were signed, usually the ones that incorporated metal work into the forms. They were signed in this manner: Pentti or P. Sarpaneva Kumela Oy. Some of his designs were later produced without metal work and were usually not signed.

Sarpaneva, Timo (Helsinki, Finland, b. 1926)

Timo Sarpaneva studied graphic design at the Central School of Industrial Design in Helsinki from 1941 to 1948. He has worked in many media, including glass, ceramics, plastics, metals, textiles, and wood. He has been designing for iittala from 1950 to the present and also for Rosenthal (Germany) on a freelance basis since 1970. Since 1988, he has worked for Venini glass (Italy) on a freelance basis.

Sarpaneva has been one of Finnish design's most prominent figures worldwide. In addition to his timeless, stylistically subdued utility glass, he is known for his impressive and ambitious glass sculptures. Sarpaneva is a master of many fields and knows his materials thoroughly. His output extends from utility and art glass to textiles, graphic art and industrial design. Timo Sarpaneva has won numerous international awards, including many Grand Prix, and gold and silver medals at the Milan Triennale. He was also awarded the Lunning Prize in 1956, as well as the Suomi Award in 1993, for a lifetime of excellence in design.

Although many of Sarpaneva's designs for iittala were signed with his complete name and company name, some were only signed with his initials, "TS", without reference to the company.

Sestervik, Lars (Sweden, b.1958)

Lars Sestervik Studied at the Industrial Arts School from 1980 to 1984. He has been a designer for Lindshammar since 1987. He has also designed series of art glass and functional glassware for the German firm Schott Zweisel.

Siiroinen, Erkkitapio (Finland, 1944-1996)

Erkkitapio (E.T.) Siiroinen completed his studies in the Department of Metal design at the University of Industrial Arts in Helsinki in 1968. In 1966, while at the University, he won a design competition sponsored by Riihimaen Lasi. By 1968, he was employed by Riihimaen Lasi as a glass designer, remaining with them until 1976. He also worked at the glass company Studiolasi Oy in 1978 and at Napapiirin Taidelasi from 1982 to 1986. From 1992 to 1996, he worked for iittala.

His designs for Riihimaen Lasi were mostly molded and cast, of complex forms which often integrated diverse geometric constructs. Some of his designs for the glassworks include the "Kasperi" series (1970), a number of mold blown forms with flower-like protuberances, and the "Pablo" series (ca. 1970), a number of mold blown vessels with circular diamond-like protuberances.

Many of E.T. Siiroinen's designs for Riihimaen Lasi were unsigned and only labeled. However, some of his hand-blown art glass designs are signed in this manner: Erkki Siiroinen Riihimaen Lasi Oy.

Sjogren, Christer (Sweden, b. 1926)

Christer Sjogren studied at Konstfack, the School of Arts, Crafts and Design from 1947 to 1951, and then worked mostly as a sculptor. He has been employed as a glass designer for Lindshammar since 1963, and continues to work there. Christer Sjogren's work can be seen at the Swedish National Museum in Stockholm, the Musee du Verre in Liege, Belgium, the Haaretz Museum in Tel Aviv, and a number of other museums both in Sweden and abroad.

Still, Nanny (Finland, b. 1926)

Nanny Still trained at the Institute of Industrial Arts from 1945 to 1949, and joined Riihimaen Lasi in 1949, where she remained until 1976. She has worked in different media such as glass, metal, pottery, ceramics, jewelry, plastics, and light fittings. In 1966 and 1968, she worked for Val St. Lambert (Belgium) in glass and ceramics production. From 1978 to the present, she has worked for Rosenthal (Germany) in glass and ceramic design. Since 1987 she has also worked for Hackman designing cookware.

Nanny Still can be described as one of the most versatile and creative personalities in Finnish design. While at Riihimaen Lasi, she created a wide range of wares, including the "Harlekiini" tableware (1958), the "Koristepullo" bottle pitchers (1959), "Saturnus" vases (1961), the "Flilandri" series (1963), the "Pompadour" vases (1968), and the "Grapponia" series (1968).

Stock, Renate (Krems, Austria, b. 1950)

Renate Stock was educated at the Austrian Fashion and Textile School of Arts and Crafts. She moved to Sweden and settled in Kosta in 1984. After completing her glass education, she has been employed at Sea Glasbruk in Kosta since 1989, where she works as a designer and product developer.

Strand, Rune (Sweden, 1924-2000)

Rune Strand belonged to a glassblowing family and learned early the techniques of glass handicraft from his father. His family moved between several glass factories which gave him experience and impulses from Swedish as well as Danish glass making tradition. During the 1960s, Strand worked for Strombergshyttan. Many of his designs for the company were engraved. Some of his designs were signed with his last name, company name and production number. He also worked at Kosta for ten years with Vicke Lindstrand.

After 1978, Strand was employed at Sea Glasbruk as a glass designer until his death in 2000. Some of his designs for Sea Glasbruk include the "Pauline" series (designed in 1983, pieces added in 1994) and the "Blomknyte" series (designed in 1978, pieces added in 1991 and 1992).

Tinback, Klas-Goran (Sweden, b. 1951)

From 1976 to 1981, Klas-Goran Tinback collaborated as glass designer for Kosta Boda Glassworks. In 1982, he spent a year as designer for Orrefors Glassworks and later established his own studio at the beautiful castle of Sturehov. Since 2000, Tinback has joined the designer team at Mat Jonasson Maleras where he, together with the two master glassblowers Jon Beyer and Ronny Fagerstrom, have created some magnificent and complex studio glass series, many with colored underlays. These include the "Two-in-one" series, the "Caribbean Blue" series, the "Navarra" series, and the "Fragancia" series.

Toikka, Oiva (Viipuri, Finland, b. 1931)

Toikka studied at the Institute of Industrial Art in Helsinki (De-

partment of Ceramics, 1953 to 1956, and Department of Art Education, 1956 to 1960). He was employed from 1956 to 1959 as a ceramist for Arabia, and also for Marimekko, the Finnish textile company in 1959. In 1963 he became a glass designer for Nuutajarvi. He was awarded the Lunning Prize in 1970. Toikka designs both household glass as well as unique art glass. Examples of his production are "Kastehelmi" (Dewdrop), "Flora," and "Fauna." To decorate glass he often uses gold or platinum particles fused in glass. In 1973, he was appointed art director of Nuutajarvi glass. Oiva Toikka has received numerous distinguished awards for his work, both in Finland and abroad.

Many of Toikka's designs for Nuutajarvi were signed in this manner: Oiva Toikka Nuutajarvi Notsjo or O. Toikka, with the company name.

Tynell, Helena (Aanekoski, Finland, b. 1918)

Helena Tynell studied design at the College of Design in Helsinki from 1938 to 1942. She was employed from 1943 to 1946 as a ceramics designer at Arabia. From 1946 to 1976, she was one of the main glass designers at Riihimaen Lasi. She was also a freelance glass designer for other companies such as Flygsfors from 1967 to 1970, and Fostoria glass in West Virginia, USA, from 1970 to 1976.

Throughout her career as a glass designer, Helena Tynell has explored most of the techniques associated with the art. Her early designs for Riihimaen Lasi included simple and sculptural blown glass forms, some undecorated and some decorated with glass engravings and glass cuttings. In 1946, she designed the "Kaulus-Sarja" vases, cylindrical forms with flared and exaggerated rims decorated with a cut linear design, very similar to Tapio Wirkkala's

Master glassblower Eelis Kankainen and Professor Oiva Toikka.

Photo by Timo Kauppila courtesy of iittala.

"Kantarelli" vase. In 1947 she designed the "Merivouko" vase, an eccentric form with a series of octopus-like tentacles around the rim, resembling a sea anemone.

During the 1950s, Tynell created some spectacular engravings in clear glass, such as "Sirkus" (Circus, 1956) and "Kissa" (Cat, 1957). In 1959 and the early 1960s, Tynell explored cut glass with colored underlays and created sculptural forms such as the "Revontulet" vase (1956) and the "Castello" series (1961). During the late 1960s and 1970s, when the demand for lower costs and mass production grew stronger, Tynell designed a series of molded wares, without compromising her artistic vision and integrity. Some of these designs include the "Kaapikello" vases (1967), "Aurinko" bottle vases (1962), and the "Piironki" vases (1974).

Vallien, Bertil (Stockholm, Sweden, b. 1938)

Bertil Vallien studied art at Konstfack, the School of Arts, Crafts, and Design, graduated at top of his class in 1961, and was awarded a Royal foundation scholarship. The grant enabled him to travel extensively in the USA and Mexico between 1961 and 1963 and, in California, to achieve his first success as a ceramics artist. On his return to Sweden, now married to his wife Ulrica, a fellow graduate of the School of Arts, Crafts and Design, Bertil moved to the glass-making region of Smaland and established himself at Afors in 1963.

Vallien immediately began to work in glass and wrought iron, and soon began to experiment with sand casting. These experiments resulted in boat-like sculptures such as "Destination X" (1986) and "Precious Cargo" (1985-1986). During the 1970s, Afors introduced the "Artists Collection" for which many of Vallien's designs were selected, in limited editions. These designs were often marketed under the Boda and Kosta Boda name, which were also part of the Afors group of glass factories. Counted among some of his most popular works is tableware such as the "Chateau" series (1981), the best-selling hand-made series of all time, with, to date, over 12 million glasses sold worldwide. Other modern classics include "Satellite" (1992), "Domino" (1993), "Viewpoints" (1995), "Tower" (1995), "Chicko" (1996) and "Brains" (1998).

Vesanto, Erkki (Finland, 1915-1990)

Erkki Vesanto studied at the Central School of Industrial Arts in Helsinki from 1933 to 1935. Vesanto was a resident designer for iittala from 1936 to 1980. Besides creating functional tableware, he created art glass pieces such as the "Lappi" series (1958). He also designed vases, some in clear glass and in transparent yellow glass with modernistic and stylized engraved decorations. One of his design characteristics is a heavy indentation in the bottom of his wares, creating a conical form and an unusual optical effect.

His designs for iittala were usually signed "Erkki Vesanto" with the design number.

Wahlstrom, Ann (Stockholm, Sweden, b. 1957)

Ann Wahlstrom studied ceramics at Capellagarden in Oland, Sweden in 1977 and 1978. In 1979, she studied at both the Glass School at Orrefors and the Pilchuck Glass School in Washington Sate. She continued her studies in 1980 at the Rhode Island School of Design under the tutelage of Dale Chihuly. In 1981 and 1982, she attended the National College of Crafts, Arts, and Design in Stockholm.

From 1982 to 1986, Wahlstrom worked as a studio glass designer in Sweden, Switzerland and the United States. Since 1986, she has been employed at Kosta Boda as a glass designer, but she has also worked in other media such as ceramics for Boda Nova (1988) and Ikea (1993), metals for Capellini International (1992), and textiles. Some of Ann Wahlstrom's designs for Kosta Boda include the "Hot Pink" series in 2000, a number of vessels with vibrant colors cased in opaque white glass with a clear glass ribbed exterior, and the "Nest" series in 2002, comprised of vessels with a linear or mottled design.

Ann Wahlstrom's designs for Kosta Boda are usually signed in this manner: A. Wahlstrom Kosta Boda with the production number.

Warff (Wolff), Ann (Germany, b. 1937)

Ann Warff worked at Pukeberg from 1959 to 1964, where she met her husband Goran Warff. From 1964 to 1978, she worked at Kosta and Kosta Boda. Until their divorce in 1972, most of her work at Kosta and Kosta Boda was in collaboration with her husband. While Goran designed many of the forms, Ann created most of the decoration, including engraving.

Collaborative designs at Kosta and Kosta Boda were usually signed "Warff," without any first names or initials. During the mid-1960s, the Warffs created a series of pieces in the "Brava" technique, where glass was poured into a mold with fragments of glass, and it would set and create a form with a heavily textured surface. Her designs at Kosta Boda include the "Snowball" candleholders (1973), one of the most commercially successful designs in the company, still produced today. In 1968, the Warffs were awarded the Lunning Prize in recognition of their work.

Warff, Goran (The Island of Gotland, Sweden, b. 1933)

From 1959 to 1964, Goran Warff worked for Pukeberg, where he met his wife and design partner Ann. Since 1964 he has worked for Kosta Boda, except for some years in 1974 to 1978 when he lived in Australia and from 1982 to 1985 when he moved to England to teach at the Sunderland Polytechnic. In 1968 the Warffs where awarded the Lunning Prize for their excellence in design.

During their employment as designer at Kosta and Kosta Boda, Goran and Ann Warff experimented greatly with the properties of glass. After their divorce in 1972, the form of his designs became quite sculptural, many with cut surfaces. Some examples of his work at Kosta include, "Caesar" vases (1985), the "Contra" series (1988), and the "Sails" series (1989).

Most of Goran Warff's designs for Kosta Boda are signed "G. Warff", distinguishing them from collaborative efforts with Ann Warff, which were often signed "Warff".

Wirkkala, Tapio (Hanko, Finland, 1915-1985)

Tapio Wirkkala studied sculpture and graphic design at the Institute of Industrial Arts in Helsinki from 1933 to 1935. From 1951 to 1954, he was the Institute's Artistic Director. Wirkkala is widely recognized as one of the most influential and multi-talented personalities in Finnish design. His works cover many areas and media, including glass, ceramics, wood, cutlery, lighting, exhibition design, graphic design, and banknote design. From 1946 to 1985, he was employed as designer for iittala and Karhula. From 1956 to 1985 he was also employed as a ceramist and glass designer for Rosenthal (Germany). From 1959 to 1985 he also designed glass for Venini (Italy).

Wirkkala was a great observer of nature, where he found much of the inspiration for his designs. Many times he would capture images with his camera and later explore them as themes in his designs. Some of his memorable designs for Karhula and iittala include the "Kantarelli" vase (1946), the "Tapio" tableware (1952) with his signature open and suspended bubble in the bases, the "Tokyo" vase (1954), with the inserted bubble design, and the "Ultima Thule" tableware (1968).

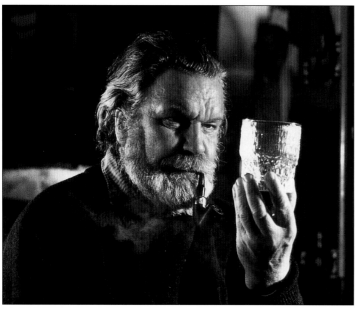

Tapio Wirkkala.

Photo courtesy of iittala.

Wirkkala, Tauno (Finland, 1917-2005)

Tauno Wirkkala studied sculpture at the Institute of Industrial Arts in Helsinki around 1945. He worked as a glass designer for Humppila Glassworks from 1971 until production was ceased at the company around 1987. Concurrently, he also worked as a glass designer for Muurla Glassworks, beginning in 1976.

Tauno Wirkkala was the younger brother of designer Tapio Wirkkala. Tauno Wirkkala's and also Humppila's most notable design is the "Revontulet" or "Northern Lights" series which was produced from 1972 to 1987. The cast forms in this series were decorated with an external number of lines or rays, and were often produced in combinations of colors.

Many, although not all of Tauno Wirkkala's designs for Humppila were signed in this manner: Tauno Wirkkala Humppila Finland.

Labels and Signatures

As a rule, Scandinavian glass was signed or marked in some fashion. Having said that, the old adage, "rules are meant to be broken," often applies. Some companies, such as Gullaskruf and Aseda, used attached paper labels and rarely signed their wares. The ones that did, such as Kosta and Orrefors, often changed their identification systems many times over the years. The following pictures and descriptions of labels, signatures, and markings are meant to serve the collector as a guide to identifying the different ways in which Scandinavian companies cataloged their wares.

Although it is by no means a complete list, we hope that it helps collectors in the correct identification of companies and artists. This list should be used in conjunction with the rest of the information provided in the book, especially the captions for the wares. We have included signatures and labels associated with the pieces in the captions. The company histories and designer biographies should also provide helpful information with identification, especially in approximating periods of production.

Labels

AFORS

Afors, Sweden (gold and yellow foil label with lion)

ALSTERBRO

Alsterbro Sweden (black and white half circles on cellophane)

ALSTERFORS

Alsterfors Sweden (blue and white paper label with a star)

Alsterfors Sweden (silver and clear cellophane label with a glassblower)

ARABIA

Arabia Wartsila Finland (black and white paper label with a crown. Arabia labels are sometimes found in Nuutajarvi's glass items. Arabia is the counterpart pottery company to Nuutajarvi Notsjo glass.)

ASEDA

Aseda Sweden (gray and white paper label)

Aseda Sweden (gray and white paper label)

Svensk Form Bo Borgstrom Sweden Aseda (black and silver foil paper label with a glass-blower figure, in the shape of the "A")

Aseda Sweden (blue and gold foil paper label with a crown and cross symbol). This is the same symbol used by Skruf in the1960s and 1970s. This label was likely used after the amalgamation of 5 Smalands glassworks in1975, (Aseda, Bjorkshult, Gullaskruf, Maleras, and Skruf), to create Royal Krona (Krona-BrukenAB). Royal Krona went bankrupt in 1977, but some of the independent glassworks survived.

BERGDALA

BJORKSHULT

Bergdala Sweden (dark blue and white paper label)

Bjorkshult Sweden (blue and white paper)

Bjorkshult Sweden (blue and white paper)

BODA

Bjorkshult Sweden (green and gold foil)

Handmade Boda Sweden (black and white paper)

Boda Sweden Erik Hoglund (black and white paper label)

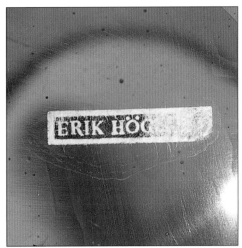

Boda Handmade Sweden (black and white paper label)

Erik Hoglund (black and white paper)

Dansk Designs Ltd. Made in Sweden GC (green and gold foil paper label, Gunnar Cyren design (GC))

DANSKEHOF

DENBY

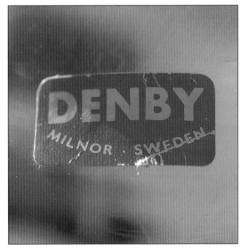

Dansk International Design (black and clear cellophane label)

Danskehof (white on clear cellophane)

Denby Milnor Sweden (red and white paper)

EKENAS

Denby Milnor

Ekenas Sweden Designer Lake (black and silver foil paper label, 1950s)

Ekenas Sweden (blue and gray round paper label with trees)

237

Ekenas Sweden (blue and gray round paper label with trees)

ELME

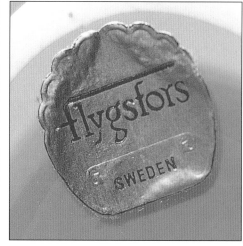

Elme

FLYGSFORS

Flygsfors Sweden (shell-shaped, red and gold foil paper label)

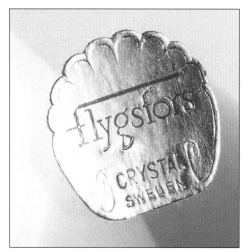

Flygsfors Crystal Sweden (shell-shaped, red and gold foil paper label)

GLIMMA

Glimma Konstglas (red, green, and silver foil paper with eagle)

Glimma Glasbruk Sweden (silver and gold foil paper circle and rectangle)

GOLDEN CROWN

Golden Crown E & R Sweden (black and white import label for Aseda)

GOTLANDSHYTTAN

Gotlandshyttan (gold on yellow paper)

GULLASKRUF

Gullaskruf Sweden (yellow and gold foil paper label)

HADELAND

Raymor, Modern in the Tradition of Good Taste 5419 RUV (RUV is the code Raymor importers used for pieces manufactured by Gullaskruf)

Hadeland Norsk Krystall (yellow and gold round foil paper label)

Hadeland Norway (black and silver foil paper label with a stylized "H")

HOLMEGAARD & KASTRUP

Hadeland Pasco Norway (round black and gold foil paper label)

Holmegaard Glas. Made in Denmark. (Danish, red and white round paper label with a swan, and round export label)

Holmegaard Glass Made in Denmark by Appointment to his Majesty the King of Denmark (red and white round paper with a swan and a crown)

Holmegaard Glass of Copenhagen by Appointment to the Royal Danish Court Made in Denmark 369 (white, black, gold and red square label with a crown and a Danish flag)

Kastrup Glas (round silver foil paper label with a Fleur de Lis)

Kastrup Glas Made in Denmark (blue and white paper label with a Fleur de Lis)

HOVMANTHORP

HUMPPILA

Kastrup-Holmegaard by Appointment to HM the King of Denmark Made in Denmark (blue and white paper label with white swan and crown)

Hovmantorp Sweden (green and white paper label)

Humppila Finland (red rays, blue cross)

IFP

Humppila Finland (silver rays, blue cross)

Humppila Finland (white rays, blue cross)

IFP Hand Made Sweden (blue and white paper label)

ILLUMS BOLIGHUS

IITTALA & KARHULA

Illums Bolighus (blue and silver foil paper oval retailer label)

Karhula (silver foil paper label with a bear, pre-1957)

i Made in Finland (red and white cellophane label, first utilized in the i-collection by Timo Sarpaneva in 1956 and later adopted as Standard label)

JOHANSFORS

Johansfors Sweden (yellow and gold foil paper label with a glassblower)

JOHANSSON

Johansson (red and silver oval foil)

KALMAR

Kalmar Sweden (red and silver foil paper)

KOSTA & KOSTA BODA

Kosta Sweden 1742 (round yellow and gold foil paper label)

Kosta Sweden (crown shaped, blue and silver foil paper label)

Kosta Sweden (black and gold cellophane label with a crown)

Kosta Boda Sweden Limited Edition by Bertil Vallien (black and silver foil paper label)

Kosta Boda c. Kosta Boda AB, Sweden Handmade (black and silver foil paper label)

Kosta Boda since 1742 (black and clear cellophane label)

KUMELA

Kumela Riihimaki Made in Finland (black and gold foil paper label with a glassblower)

LINDSHAMMAR

Lindshammar Sweden Gunnar Ander (black, blue and white paper label with an "L", specific to Gunnar Ander designs. The same label can be found for other designers.)

Lindshammars Made in Sweden for Partial Fostoria Label. (During the 1970s, the American company, Fostoria, commissioned pieces from Lindshammar which were sold as part of the Fostoria line.)

Handmade in Sweden by Lindshammar (paper label with blue and yellow Swedish flag)

MAGNOR

Magnor Glass Norway (black and white oval paper label)

MALERAS

Maleras Glas Made in Sweden (black and silver foil paper label)

MANTHORP (HOVMANTHORP)

Mantorp Sweden (dark brown and white paper label)

MATS JONASSON MALERAS

Company logo in white on black, also used for label.

NUUTAJARVI NOTSJO

Nuutajarvi Notsjo 1793 Suomi Finland (black and white cellophane label with a stylized fish)

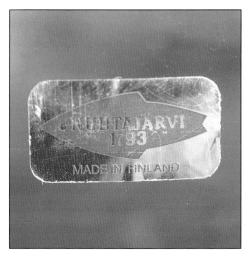

ORREFORS

PUKEBERG

Nuutajarvi 1793 Made in Finland (blue and silver cellophane label with stylized fish)

Orrefors Sweden (brown and white, shield label with rooster)

Pukeberg Sweden (yellow and silver foil paper label)

RANDSFJORDGLASS
(RANDSFJORD GLASSWORKS)

Pukeberg Sweden (black and white cellophane label)

Randsfjordglass Made in Norway Handblown (red and gold foil paper label)

Randsfjordglass Made in Norway Design Hanna Hellum.(black and white paper)

RIIHIMAEN LASI

Randsfjordglass Made in Norway Design Benny Motzfeldt (black and white paper label)

Randsfjordglass Made in Norway Design T. Torgersen (blue and white paper label)

Riihimaki Suomi Finland (red and black triangular cellophane label)

Riihimaen Lasi Made in Finland (gold and Black round cellophane label with stylized lion)

Riihimaen Lasi Made in Finland (white and clear cellophane label with a stylized lion's paw mark)

Riihimaki Finland (blue and clear cellophane label with a heart design and a small lion)

ROYAL COPENHAGEN

Finncristall Made in Finland (gold and Black cellophane label used only by Riihimaen Lasi mainly in the late 1960s and 1970s, for pieces intended for the tourist and export market.)

Riihimaki (gold foil paper with lion)

Royal Copenhagen (blue and white circle with crown)

RYD

SEA GLASBRUK

RYD Sweden (red, black and silver foil paper label. The indistinguishable upper part is simply a silver "R" letter with a red background.)

Sea Glasbruk Kosta Sweden (red and gold foil paper label, in the shape of a shield)

Sea Glasbruk AB Kosta Sweden (black and clear cellophane label)

SKRUF

Skruf Sweden Full Crystal (yellow black and gold foil paper label with a crown)

Skruf Sweden (gold, black and clear cellophane label, with a cross and a crown)

SMALANDSHYTTAN

Smalandshyttan Sweden (blue and gold foil paper label)

STROMBERGSHYTTAN

Strombergshyttan Sweden (silver and black cellophane label)

STUDIOGLAS STROMBERGSHYTTAN

Studioglas Strombergshyttan Sweden (black on cellophane).

MADE IN SWEDEN

Made in Sweden (round gold foil paper label)

Swedish glass (green and silver foil paper label with 3 stars)

Swedish Art Glass (black and silver foil on paper oval)

Swedish Glass (green and gold foil paper with three stars)

245

Signatures

AFORS

Afors G.H. 554 E. Gordon (Afors company signature, Ernest Gordon code and production code, and Ernest Gordon signature)

BODA

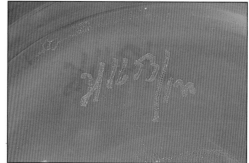

H and model number (Erik Hoglund for Boda). Most Boda pieces designed by Hoglund have only an "H," without a reference to "Boda" in the marking.

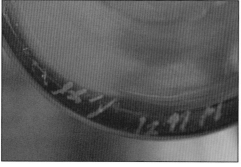

H and model number (Erik Hoglund for Boda)

EKENAS

Ekenas Sweden L1456-17 J. O. Lake (Ekenas company signature, production number, and John Orwar Lake signature)

Ekenas Sweden L1462-17 J. O. Lake (Ekenas company signature, production number, and John Orwar Lake signature)

Ekenas Sweden

FLYGSFORS

Flygsfors-56 (Flygsfors company signature and production year)

Berndt (Wiktor Berndt signature)

Coquille (Coquille range)

GULLASKRUF

Blomberg Gullaskruf 1963 (Kjell Blomberg signature, Gullaskruf company signature, year of production)

HALLINGLASS

Hallingsglass Norway (Hallinglass company signature and designer name)

HOLMEGAARD & KASTRUP

Holmegaard 19PL55 (Holmegaard company signature and production date with Per Lutken initials)

Holmegaard 1955 (Holmegaard company signature and production date)

Holmegaard 19PL60 KH (Holmegaard company signature, production date with Per Lutken's initials, and Kastrup Holmegaard engraved initials)

HOVMANTHORP

Hovmantorp Sweden 1007 (Hovmantorp company signature and production number)

HUMPPILA

Pertti Santalahti

Humppila Finland

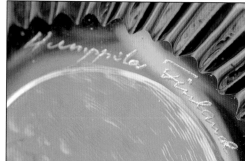

Humppila Finland

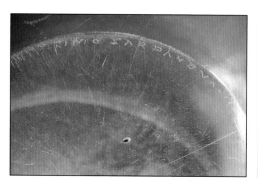

Tauno Wirkkala

IITTALA & KARHULA

G Hongell- Karhula (Goran Hongell signature and Karhula company signature)

Timo Sarpaneva- iittala (Timo Sarpaneva Signature and iittala company signature)

Tapio Wirkkala (Tapio Wirkkala signature and illegible production number)

JOHANSFORS

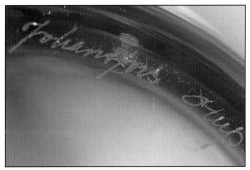

Johansfors Orup (Johansfors company signature and Bengt Orup signature)

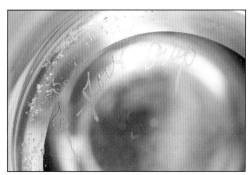

J.fors Orup (Johansfors company signature and Bengt Orup signature)

KALMAR

Kalmar signature and production number. Pieces are often signed T. Pors (Tora Pors).

KOSTA & KOSTA BODA

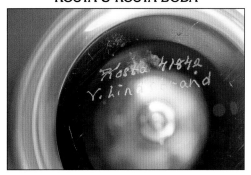

Kosta 41842 V. Lindstrand (Kosta company signature, 5-digit production number (1970s and after), and Vicke Lindstrand signature)

Kosta LH 1717 (Kosta company signature, Vicke Lindstrand [initial (L), type of glass (H for "blown")], and digit production number (pre-1970s))

Kosta 48254 Tinback (Kosta company signature, 5-digit production number (1970s), Klas-Goran Tinback signature)

Kosta 56129 Warff (Kosta company signature, 5-digit production number, Ann and Goran Warff signature)

Kosta Boda M. Backstrom Atelje (Kosta Boda signature, Monica Backstrom signature and Atelje marking, which was used in limited edition pieces)

Kosta Boda 48860 G. Warff (Kosta Boda company signature, 5-digit production number, Goran Warff signature)

Kosta Boda G. Warff 49808 (Kosta Boda company signature, Goran Warff signature and 5 digit production number)

KUMELA

Armando Jacobino (Armando Jacobino for Kumela)

Kai Blomqvist (Kai Blomqvist for Kumela)

NUUTAJARVI NOTSJO

K.F. Nuutajarvi Notsjo-61 (Kaj Frank initials, Nuutajarvi Notsjo company signature, and production year)

I. Toikka Nuutajarvi (Inkeri Toikka signature and Nuutajarvi company signature)

ORREFORS

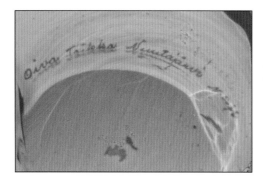

Oiva Toikka (Oiva Toikka and Nuutajarvi company signature)

Orrefors NU 3538/1 (Orrefors company signature, "N", Nils Landberg designer code and "U" for "blown glass worked in the blowing room," and production number)

Orrefors Sweden (Molded Orrefors company signature found in Colora bowls designed by Sven Palmqvist

Orrefors (stamped company signature)

Orrefors Graal Nr. 234 S Edward Hald (Orrefors company signature, Graal technique, production number, and Edward Hald signature)

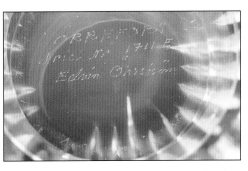

Orrefors Ariel Nr. 1711 E Edwin Ohrstrom (Orrefors company signature, Ariel technique, production number, and Edwin Ohrstrom signature)

PLUS GLASSHYTTE

Plus Norway (Plus Glasshytte company acid etched mark. Note that a plus sign is created between the "[ ]" marking)

RIIHIMAEN LASI

Riihimaen Lasi O.Y. Tamara Aladin (Riihimaen Lasi company signature and Tamara Aladin signature)

Riihimaen Lasi O.Y. Nanny Still (Riihimaen Lasi company signature and Nanny Still signature)

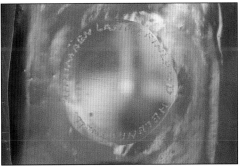

Riihimaen Lasi O.Y. Finland Helena Tynell (Riihimaen Lasi company signature and Helena Tynell signature)

Riihamaen Lasi (circle seal with lion)

Sea Glasbruk signature.

SKRUF

530 Bengt Edenfalk (production number and Bengt Edenfalk signature)

Skruf Sweden (Skruf company acid etched mark with cross and crown)

STROMBERGSHYTTAN

Stromberg (B845) (Strombergshyttan company signature and production code—not designer-specific.)

Strombergshyttan [B426] (Strombergshyttan company signature and production code)

STUDIO STROMBERGSHYTTAN

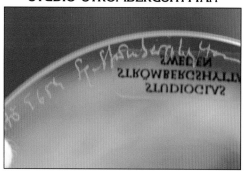

Studio Strombergshyttan signature

TRANSJO

Transjo Sweden company signature

Selected Bibliography

Aav, Marianne & Nina Stritzler-Levine. *Finnish Modern Design: Utopian Ideals and Everyday Realities, 1930-1997*. Yale University Press: London, 1998.

Arrhenius, Lilly. *Svensk Heminredning – Swedish Design*. Vepe Forlag Bokindustri AB: Stockholm, 1957.

Arts Council of Finland and Finnish Ministry of Education. *Design 2005 – Government Decision-In-Principle on Finnish Design Policy* 15.06.2000. Arts Council of Finland and Finnish Ministry of Education: Helsinki, 2000.

Auktion for Svenskt Konstglas. *Auktionsverket* auction catalog, Stockholm, August 4, 1985.

Auktion for Svenskt Konstglas. *Auktionsverket* auction catalog, Stockholm, August 8, 1987.

Axelsson, Rune B. *Swedish Glass-Awarded Design*. National Swedish Industrial Board: Stockholm, 1984.

Beard, Geoffrey. *International Modern Glass*. Charles Scribner's Sons: New York, 1976.

_____. *Modern Glass*. Studio Vista Limited: Great Britain, 1968.

Brown, Conrad. "Coming: Revolution in Scandinavian Design". Craft Horizons, March-April 1958.

The Corning Museum of Glass. *Glass 1959: A Special Exhibition of International Contemporary Glass*. The Corning Museum of Glass: New York, 1959.

Dahlback, Helena & Marianne Uggla. *The Lunning Prize*. Risbergs Tryckeri AB: Stockholm, 1986.

Dawson, Jack. *Finnish Post-War Glass: 1945-1996*. University of Sunderland: UnitedKingdom, 1988.

Ellison, Michael & Leslie Piña. *Scandinavian Modern Furnishings 1930-1970: Designed for Life*. Atglen, PA: Schiffer, 2002.

Fiell, Charlotte & Peter Fiell. *50's Decorative Art*. Benedikt Taschen Verlag GmbH: Koln, 2000.

_____. *60's Decorative Art*. Benedikt Taschen Verlag GmbH: Koln, 2000.

_____. *70's Decorative Art*. Benedikt Taschen Verlag GmbH: Koln, 2000.

Finnish Glass Museum, The. *Finnish Glass – Glass Manufacturers' Brochures from the 1950's*. Riihimaki, 2000

_____. *Make Glass Not War: Finnish Glass from the 1960's*. Finnish Glass Museum, 1992.

The Finnish Society of Crafts and Design. *Tapio Wirkkala*. The Finnish Society of Crafts and Design: Helsinki, 1985.

Form, Function, Finland. Issue. 79-80, Volume 3-4/2000

Gerstenberg, Susanne & John Amott. "Bengt Edenfalk", 1991. Catalog with a brief presentation of Bengt Edenfalk's artistry.

Grover, Ray & Lee Grover. *Contemporary Art Glass*. New York, NY: Crown Publishers, 1975.

Harrison Beer, Eileene. *Scandinavian Design: Objects of a Life Style*. New York, NY: Farrar Straus and Giroux, 1975.

Hawkins Opie, Jennifer. *Scandinavia- Ceramics & Glass in the Twentieth Century*. Rizzoli International Publications: New York, 1990.

Helena Tynell Design 1943-1993. The Finnish Glass Museum: Finland, 1998.

The Helsinki City Art Museum. *Timo Sarpaneva: A Retrospective*. The Helsinki City Art Museum: Finland.

Holmer, Gunnel. *The Brilliance of Swedish Glass: 1918-1939*. The Bard Graduate Center for Studies in the Decorative Arts: New York, 1996.

Important 20th Century Glass: The Hal Metzler Collection. Christie's auction catalog, Chicago, May 16, 1998.

iittala Glass Museum. *Alvar and Aino Aalto as Glass Designers*. Exhibition catalog, 1988.

Italian Design. Christie's auction catalog, South Kensington, June 3. 1998.

Jackson, Lesley. *20th Century Factory Glass*. Rizzoli Publications: New York, 2000.

Jantunen, Paivi, Kaj Martin, & Liisa Rasanen. *Oiva Toikka: Glass from Nuutajarvi*. Exhibition Catalog: Amos Anderson Art Museum.

Kahma, Marketta. *The Modern Spirit: Glass from Finland*. Vientipaino Oy: Helsinki, 1985.

Kastrup & Holmegaard Glassworks. *150 Years of Danish Glass*. Exhibition catalog. Caulfield Institute of Technology, Melbourne.

Katonah Gallery. *Art by Design: Reflections of Finland*. New York: Katonah Gallery, 1988.

Koivisto, Kaisa. *Suomen Lasi Elaa: Finnish Glass Lives*. The Finnish Glass Museum: Finland,1986.

Kosta Boda – 8 Individuals. Rahms I Lund tryckeri AB: Lind, 1991.

The Kosta Boda Book of Glass. Current Collection as of June 1, 1986. Strokirks: Sweden.

"Kumela - lasimaalaamosta tehtaaksi ja Humppila - lasitehdas tien varrella." *Suomen Lasimuseo*. 2002. www.kunta.riihimaki.fi/Lasimus/Kumela_Humppila.

Lassen, Erik & Mogens Schluter. *Dansk Glass 1925-1985*. Nyt Nordisk Forlag Arnold Busck: Copenhagen, 1987.

Lutken, Per. *Glass is Life*. Holmegaard Glassworks, Royal Copenhagen A/S, and Nyt Nordisk Forlag Arnold Busck: Copenhagen, 1986.

Lutzeier, Sabine. *Modernes Glas Von 1920-1990*. Battenberg Verlag Augsburg: Austria, 1993.

Modernes Design. Quittenbaum auction catalog, Munchen, March 20, 2000.

Modernes Design – Kunsthandwerk Nach 1945. Quittenbaum auction catalog, Munchen, November 18, 2000.

Modern Design. Phillip's auction catalog, New York, March 20, 1999.

Modern Design. Christie's auction catalog, South Kensington, October 7, 1998.

Museum of Art and Design. *Tapio Wirkkala: Eye, Hand, Thought*. Museum of Art and Design: Helsinki 2000.

Nanny Still. Suomen Lasimuseo: Finland, 1996.

New Scandinavian Glass. Exhibition catalog. Ten Arrow Gallery, Massachusetts, March 20 to April 15, 1978.

New Scandinavian Glass. Exhibition catalog. Ten Arrow Gallery, Massachusetts, May 12 to June 7, 1980.

Orvola, Mirja. *Craft Design: Heikki Orvola*. Kustannus Pohjoinen: Finland, 2000.

A Private Collection of Finnish Design. Christie's auction catalog, March 7, 2001.

Piña, Leslie. *Fifties Glass*. Second Edition. Atglen, PA: Schiffer Publishing, Ltd., 2000.

_____. *Circa Fifties Glass*. Atglen, PA: Schiffer Publishing, Ltd., 1997.

Remlov, Arne. *Design in Scandinavia*. Kirstes Boktrykkeri: Norway, 1950's.

Ricke, Helmut & Lars Thor. *Swedish Glass Factories: Production Catalogues 1915- 1960*. Prestel-Verlag: Munchen, 1987.

Ricke, Helmut & Ulrich Gronert. *Glas in Schweden, 1915-1960*. Prestel-Verlag Munchen und Kunstmuseaum: Dusseldorf, 1986.

Robert, Guy. *Kostaglas*. Kosta Glasbruk: Sweden, 1963.

Scandinavian Design. Christie's auction catalog, South Kensington, September 15, 1999.

"Sigvard Bernadotte." *Beoworld*. 2005. www.beoworld.co.uk/bernadotte.

Skawonius, Sven Erik. *Glas for Hushallet*. Special edition of *Form*, January, 1960.

Soderstrom Osayeyhtio, Werner. *Kaj Franck: Designer*. WSOY: Porvoo, 1993.

Sparke, Penny. *A Century of Design: Design Pioneers of the 20th Century*. Barron's: New York, 1988.

Stennett-Willson, R. *The Beauty of Modern Glass*. The Studios Limited: London, 1958.

Stockholms Auktionsverk. Auction catalog. *Specialauktion-Svenskt Konstglas*. August 5, 2001.

Stromberg, Juoko. "Finish Art Glass Designers." 2004. koti.mbnet.fi/jost/index.

Sunderland Arts Centre. *Suomen Lasi – Finnish Glass*. Smith Print Group: Newcastle Upon Tyne, 1979.

Svenskt Konstglas. *Auktionsverket* auction catalog, Stockholm, August 12, 1990.

Svenskt Konstglas. *Auktionsverket* auction catalog, Stockholm, August 9, 1992.

Veneti nel Mondo. "Vetrai di Murano Nella Diaspora di Angelo Tajani,' May 2002. <http://www.regione.veneto.it/videoinf/periodic/precedenti/numero25/dallasvezia.htm>.

Vigier, Lorenzo & Leslie Piña. *Scandinavian Glass 1930-2000: Smoke & Ice*. Atglen, PA: Schiffer, 2002.

Webb, Aileen O., Rose Slivka, and Margaret Merwin Patch. *The Crafts of the Modern World*. New York: Bramhall House, 1968.

Wickman, Kerstin. *Orrefors: A Century of Swedish Glassmaking*. Byggforlaget-Kultur: Stockhom, 1998.

Widman, Dag. *Svenskt glas 1900-1960* (Swedish Glass 1900-1960). Stockholm: Bokforlaget Cordia, 1996.

Willman, Tiina. Email correspondence from 2001 to 2005.

Willman, Tiina. "Glass Art." 2002. www.glassart.5u.com/Indexe.

Zahle, Erik. *A Treasury of Scandinavian Design*. Golden Press: New York, 1961.

Company catalogs for most companies listed in the book, spanning from 1950 to 2005.

Index